Daily Comforts
for Caregivers

D1165987

Daily Comforts
for Caregivers

Pat Samples

Fairview Press
Minneapolis, Minnesota

Published by Fairview Press, 2450 Riverside Avenue South, Minneapolis, MN 55454.

Library of Congress Cataloging-in-Publication Data
Samples, Pat.
    Daily comforts for caregivers / by Pat Samples.
        p.   cm.
    Includes index.
    ISBN 1-57749-088-6 (pbk. : alk. paper)
    1. Caregivers Prayer--books and devotions--English.
   2. Devotional calendars.   I. Title
   BL625.9.C35S36   1999
   291.4'32--dc21   99-43552
                                               CIP

First Printing: October 1999

Printed in the United States of America
07   7 6

Cover: *Cover Design by Laurie Ingram Duren*™
Text design: Dorie McClelland, Spring Type & Design

For a free current catalog of Fairview Press titles, call toll-free 1-800-544-8207.

Acknowledgments

My sincere thanks to Lane Stiles and Fairview Press for asking me to write this book, and to the many caregivers whose difficulties, delights, and discoveries are reflected in its pages. I am also grateful to my friends and colleagues who have supported me in my commitment to ease the journey for caregivers. In particular, I want to thank close friends Ron Nelsen, Beverly Gerber, Linda Gearke, Bonnie Karlen, Rita Mays, and Joni and Jerry Woelfel, who cheered me on through the many long days of writing and revising and helped me keep my life in balance.

Jane Anderson and Carolyn Torp gave conscientious attention to reviewing every page of an early draft and offered wise suggestions based on their experience with caregiving. I thank them for their generosity and encouragement and for helping to assure authenticity in these pages.

My deep thanks go to Tim McIndoo, who has edited my works with extraordinary skill over the past decade and has become a treasured mentor and friend. His steady advocacy for simple writing, his insightful questioning and prompting, and his unfailing sensitivity to the message, the writer, and the reader strengthened every meditation.

I am grateful to God for the privilege of helping to bring this book into being.

Introduction:
The Comfort of Your Own Wisdom

A BOOK FOR CAREGIVERS

If you are caring for someone with chronic or long-term health problems, this book is for you. Perhaps you are caring for a spouse, relative, or friend with a deteriorating condition. You may be in the "sandwich" generation, helping out an older relative while maintaining family responsibilities. You may be raising a child or living with a sibling who has a disability. Whether the person you are caring for lives with you, at another residence, or in a care facility, this book may be helpful. It is written mostly for family members and friends, but professional caregivers should find it helpful as well.

A GUIDE TO PEACE OF MIND

As a caregiver, you have a right to peace of mind. Deep inside you is all the wisdom you need to make sound choices as you care for this special person in your life. When you tap into this wisdom, you draw on a lifetime of spiritual and practical resources to guide you. As a result, you can have peace of mind.

However, if you don't take care of yourself, you may not be able to tap into that wisdom very easily. This book will help you, day by day, to remember to take care of yourself and to stay in touch with your own wisdom.

MEDITATIONS TO LIVE BY

Each of these daily meditations is like a self-advice column. The first paragraph begins with a concern or realization commonly expressed by caregivers. The second paragraph explores the issue further and draws on the commonsense wisdom we all have when we're in our most open and effective frame of mind. It reflects the heartfelt wisdom of many caregivers like yourself who contributed to the development of this book. It suggests fresh ways to think about troubling situations and to build on your strengths. It invites you to ponder your own ways of resolving difficult problems and to appreciate the gifts that come from caregiving. If the wisdom that's offered on a given day doesn't quite fit for you, you can use it as a springboard to explore your own beliefs and insights.

At the end of each meditation is an affirmation or reflection that summarizes a key insight. You can use it for inspiration and direction throughout the day. It is written as a declaration to help you state your innermost conviction and give you the strength to live by it. By making this declaration in the present tense, you are laying claim to what you know and do in your finest moments. Feel free to reword it so that it expresses a truth you can live by.

REMEMBERING YOUR SPIRITUAL POWER

All readers of this book will have their own individual spiritual convictions. Out of respect for the diverse ways people talk about the source of their spiritual strength, this book uses the term Spiritual Power most of the time. For you, that might mean God, Allah, Great Spirit, the Tao, or whatever else sustains you from day to day—the help of friends, inspiring books or music, your "aha" moments, the beauty of nature. Substitute whatever term is helpful to you.

WAYS TO USE THIS BOOK

Each meditation matches a day on the calendar. However, you can read about a subject of your choosing rather than the day's meditation. Consult the alphabetical index in the back of the book.

Here are some suggestions for using each meditation:

Consider taking a few minutes at the beginning of your day or at some other regular time for quiet reflection. Open your heart and mind to the wisdom within you. You may wish to do this alone, or with another caregiver so you can share ideas on the topic and support each other.

Using your own form of prayer, ask for guidance in finding the wisdom that will be most helpful for you today.

Then read the meditation through.

Write down the thoughts that come to mind, as well as the feelings in your heart.

Copy down the declaration statement or create your own to help you remember the message. Consider posting it where you can see it often during the day.

To reinforce any insights you gain from this time of reflection, share them with others during the day.

Enjoy the peace of mind that comes from drawing on your own wisdom.

Promise

A new year is supposed to be a sign of promise, of hope. But I can see more problems than promise on the horizon. Considering my loved one's condition, I get scared when I think of what might happen this year. Hope seems out of reach. Yet I'd like to find a way to keep a brighter outlook.

I know that hope won't come from focusing on the uncertain nature of my loved one's situation. The truth is, I can't depend on anything "out there" to create a sense of promise. That's an inside job. It's possible I can find hope if I trust in the generosity of life. Not that I can expect any particular outcome just because I want it. But I can expect to find gifts in every situation I face, no matter how difficult the circumstances seem. My window on the world determines whether or not I notice them. I could start the year by cleaning my window and looking above the clouds.

When I let in more light, I see more promise.

Making Decisions

With all the decisions I have to make, my thinking gets stuck sometimes. Making financial arrangements, choosing the right kind of services—I get overwhelmed by all the pros and cons of the various options. I can't decide what's best.

What I've noticed is that the harder I push myself to decide, the more confused I get. If I'm not getting results, it makes sense to stop pushing for a while. I can set aside my deliberation and do something else until my mind clears, or I can sit quietly and invite my mind to become still. I can turn to my intuition or my Spiritual Power for insight and ask, What is the best solution? I let the question rest there in the quiet. I don't expect a rush answer. It will come. If I don't understand it clearly in my quiet time, I trust that the understanding will be there when I need it.

My inner wisdom comes to me
if I quiet myself and listen.

Getting Away

I've always liked to take little trips out of town to get away. But that's over with for now. I can't go anywhere and leave my loved one behind. I don't want her to feel upset because she can't go along. And I'd feel terrible if anything happened to her while I was away.

It's not that she insists I stay. She wants me to have the freedom to go have some fun. She says, "Send a postcard." I tell her I can't leave, but that's my overly responsible self speaking. I think she can't manage without me. I think I shouldn't go. I worry, What would other people think? But in truth, it would do me good to get away. Maybe she'd even like a break from me. Besides, it doesn't matter in the end what other people think. What matters is what's best for her and me. Of course, I want to make sure everything is taken care of while I'm gone, but that is doable if I make the necessary arrangements.

I'll plan a getaway today.

Jealousy

People are always asking me how my loved one is doing. I'm glad they care enough to ask. I wish sometimes they would ask about me as well. I could use a show of concern.

It seems odd that I'm feeling a little jealous over the attention being given to the person I care for. I wouldn't want to be in my loved one's shoes. Yet, although my problems might seem small by comparison, I'm having a difficult time, too. I'm not sure other people understand that. The problems my loved one experiences are more apparent than mine. If I want support for myself, I guess I have to let others know that their support is important to me. I can mention that the situation is challenging for both of us. I can ask someone to stop in to visit with me or to run an errand or say a prayer for me. By asking for support, I am honoring my own desires and showing compassion for myself.

I let others know when I want support.

Fun Times

When I have to deal with all the tough problems that arise because of my loved one's condition, it's easy for me to get bogged down in these troubles. It's easy to start feeling somber, glum.

But I don't want to forget to have fun. A little laughter helps keep my loved one and me in an upbeat frame of mind. Everyone involved in her care benefits when we quit taking everything so seriously. Of course, I wouldn't make light of her pain and struggles, especially when she's having difficult episodes. But for the most part, I keep on teasing her like I always have. I bring a few jokes into our conversation. I retell stories that keep the good times alive. And since we both fumble a lot with the ever-changing procedures involved in her care, I like to poke fun at our foibles. A little lightness keeps our struggles in perspective.

I treasure the fun times in the midst of our troubles.

Inadequate or Magnificent?

I don't always feel confident I can give the kind of care that's needed. I worry that I won't be able to figure out what I need to do. I fear I'll make a mistake. I feel responsible but inadequate for the job.

All these concerns are based in fear. But I do not have to be bound by fear. I can recognize that I am a wise, capable, and powerful person. I know there have been times when I have risen to meet some very difficult challenges and felt confident and pleased with myself. There is nothing stopping me from doing the same now. Fear is my only barrier. Perhaps I'm hanging on to the fear so I won't be asked to let my light shine brightly. Perhaps I'm afraid of my own magnificence. But I was created to live my life to the fullest and I might as well do it.

I let go of my fears and let my light shine.

Interrupted Plans

It does no good to make plans. I make appointments or arrange for an event or decide on a moving date, and then wham! A sudden turn in my loved one's situation brings everything to a halt. It makes me want to give up planning altogether.

My whole life is in flux because of his condition. I'm getting used to it, in a way. Whenever I try to schedule anything, I tell people, "Assuming nothing goes wrong...." I can't count on anything happening for certain. That puts me on edge. But of course, all plans are contingent, regardless of my loved one's condition. Everything from car problems to weather changes to computer glitches can throw off someone's plans. Uncertainty is part of life. That doesn't mean I can never plan anything, it only means I must keep myself flexible enough to make adjustments as needed.

Expecting surprises is part of my plan.

Hope or Acceptance?

There are days when I'm sure nothing more can be done for my loved one. On other days, I'm just as sure we shouldn't give up hope.

People do sometimes rally unexpectedly, even recover miraculously. Prayer and positive attitude have been known to help. New treatments are constantly being found. It makes sense to explore every possible avenue that might help improve my loved one's health. But it is also reasonable to accept the limits of his health condition. There is no absolute certainty that things will go one way or the other. Moment-by-moment attention and wisdom are called for. I peacefully accept my best understanding of the situation in each moment. Yet I remain open to new insights or information. Each perspective brings a flood of feelings to go with it. Each point of view is right in its own time.

I keep hope and acceptance in balance by paying close attention to the realities of the moment.

Affirmations

I get stuck in certain ways of doing things that I wish I could change. I worry. I avoid problems. I get angry. I give in. I don't take time to eat. There are many things I do over and over that aren't good for me or that don't match my values. I get discouraged when I try to stop doing them and then don't succeed.

If I say affirmations, though, I feel reconnected with my values and I'm reminded of how I act when I'm at my best: *I am capable. I stand up for myself. I eat what my body needs. I release my anger.* By saying affirmations such as these over and over, I redirect my thoughts. It helps if I write them out and place them around my home, car, and work area. It also helps if I declare them with feeling, even loudly, so they become embedded in my mind. Before long, they become automatic ways of believing in myself and reacting to what happens in my life.

> *Today, I will create an affirmation*
> *and say it at least five times.*

Setting Limits

I feel so responsible for my loved one that, if she asks for something, I'm tempted to drop everything and give it to her immediately. But sometimes her requests are more like demands. Or she attempts to manipulate me into doing something I don't really want to do. Then I get resentful. Yet when I don't give her what she wants, I feel guilty.

I believe in being kind, in doing things for others in need. But giving that is done out of guilt combined with resentment is hardly kind. It comes from a distorted sense of duty. Giving in to unreasonable demands shows a lack of self-respect. The truth is, I can say no to her just as kindly as I can say yes. When I do say no, I'm respecting not only myself but her ability to cope with disappointment and find other ways to get what she wants. If she keeps the pressure on even after I've said no, I don't argue. I just repeat my no while reassuring her I care about her.

By saying no, I let others know my limits.

In High Gear

They say, "God doesn't give you more than you can handle." I might argue with that. Some days a constant rush of chaos and crisis is coming at me and there's no help in sight. It's shoot from the hip—no time to aim, just draw and fire. It's react, react, react.

In those moments, I have no choice but to grab onto whatever I can—intuition, instinct, whatever you want to call it. Everything's instantaneous. Decide. Respond. Act. There is no right or wrong, just do. It's a hell that no one looking in from the outside can fully grasp, or judge fairly. I have to move—and move quickly—and nothing seems like a safe way out. I throw myself into the situation because I care and, in so doing, I stumble into the arms of a guiding Spiritual Power that takes charge. When I come out the other end, I wonder how I lived through it and I take a deep breath.

Every crisis comes with automatic Power steering.

I'm Not Doing Enough

I have to admit I'm not doing everything I could for my loved one, and some days I feel guilty about that. I feel like a failure. I keep thinking I should be doing more or that I'm not doing things well enough.

However, it's easy to forget all that I am doing as a caregiver. I handle legal and financial matters. I arrange for necessary care. I stay in close contact. I offer comfort and hands-on help and much more. I do the best I can. Today is a good day to remember how much I am giving, and appreciate myself for that. I could even look in the mirror and say, "Thank you!"

Today I will write a list of my contributions as a caregiver and feel satisfaction in what I give.

Intolerance for Suffering

No one likes to be around pain. When my loved one is hurting badly, I have a hard time being around him. Other people who aren't as close to him have an even harder time. I ask them to help out once in a while, even just to sit with him, but they either make excuses or come and squirm the whole time.

I have an easier time when he shows improvement and isn't suffering as much. When his condition is poor, I feel frustrated because I can't make it better, and I tend to feel the pain along with him. I'm sure others feel that way too, and that's why they hesitate to visit. I can't expect others to do more than they are willing to do, yet I need a break sometimes. When I ask others to come, it helps if I suggest short stays and let them know that they are not expected to come up with solutions for my loved one, only to give caring attention. I remember that for myself as well.

My job is to care, not cure.

I've Changed

I've changed since I've become a caregiver. I'm not sure exactly how, but I know I'm not the same. In fact, I'll never be the same person I was before.

That's partly a good thing. I've learned a lot. I'm stronger in certain ways. A few of my opinions have changed. I've gotten tougher in some ways, softer in others. These changes haven't come easy. I've had to give up some things along the way that mattered to me. I can't do everything I used to. It might be worthwhile to make a list of all the changes I see in myself. That way I can celebrate the gains and mourn the losses. I can mark the milestones and know where I'm starting from today. I'll know myself better.

Today I will note at least three changes I have made and notice how I feel as I allow them to sink in.

Protection vs. Participation

I try to protect my loved one from any more pain and difficulty than necessary. That's why I don't tell her much when something goes wrong or when I'm having a hard time. I don't want to worry her. I carry the burdens for both of us.

I wonder if I'm being overprotective. If I carry the burden alone, am I keeping us from sharing a part of this journey together? I want to be sensitive to her fragile condition, but I also want to respect her capabilities. I don't want to do for her what she could do for herself. By not allowing her to participate in dealing with the daily challenges happening around us, I may be denying her full participation in life. If I tell her about my concerns, she may feel relieved to be involved and enjoy helping as much as she can. By making a contribution, she won't feel so left out or feel like she is only a burden to me. And I won't have to be so strong all the time.

A shared load is lighter.

Questioning My Faith

It doesn't seem fair. I don't understand why my loved one has to suffer like this. At times like these I'm tempted to question my faith. How could a caring God let something like this happen?

I'm surprised by how angry I get about this. My strong reaction makes me a little anxious. I never thought I'd have doubts about my faith, especially when I need it the most. But my patience has run out. I want things to be different. I've prayed the best way I know how and nothing seems to get better. But even though I can justify my getting angry, it doesn't give me any answers either. Maybe I never will fully understand the "why" of this. It seems that's just how life is. There is suffering, whether I like it or not. What matters is how I deal with it. Maybe that's where God or some other Spiritual Power comes in—helping me by walking with me through my anger.

I trust I will find my way
through my anger and doubt.

Private Life

My life is not as private these days. Professional helpers are around a lot. People we barely know are asking us questions, entering into our private matters, and making decisions that affect our lives. It is uncomfortable to be under so much scrutiny.

Having other people around so much is taking some getting used to. It might help if I let them know how they can support my desire for privacy. I can also look for ways to *feel* private when that's important to me. One way is to close my eyes or step into another room. Another is to refuse to give information I prefer not to reveal. But I can also look for ways to widen my acceptance of others into my personal territory. Perhaps opening my heart a little will help. If I examine my fears about having others so close to me, I may be able to gradually relax them.

> *I make more room in my heart for others*
> *who help my loved one.*

Silence

The silence gets to me sometimes. I just sit and wait and there isn't anything to say. My loved one is asleep or can't communicate. No one is around to talk with, and no words matter much anyway in this situation. The silence is agonizingly empty.

What if, just for today, I embraced the silence as something sacred? As a gift? As something to treasure? If I become willing to step into the emptiness that silence offers, I may be able to enter a deep, holy place inside myself where there is no need for sound or activity. In that still, sacred center of my being, I may find a sense of peace and reassurance more eloquent and soothing than words.

I rest in the sanctity of the silence.

Smiles

I force a smile some days when I go to spend time with my loved one. I may feel discouraged or sad or annoyed, but I smile nonetheless. I want to bring as much comfort and pleasantness as I can to my loved one. Also it's harder for me to stay down in the dumps when I have a smile on my face.

I'm surprised by how much a smile can lift my spirits—and lift hers, too. By smiling when I don't feel like it, I'm practicing being happy. I know that at times I'm able to change some behaviors and feelings by acting as if the change has already happened. I create an intention in my mind about the way I want to be and then practice it. A smile is my practice for happiness. It reminds me that I'm willing to be happy, that underneath the troubles in my life I have a deep belief that there is much kindness and love in the universe.

I am willing to be happy and I practice by smiling.

Survival

Sometimes people say, "All he needs is love and everything will be okay." But it's not that simple. Yes, love is important, but it's not a magic pill. It doesn't take away all the history or the pain or the impossible behaviors. Loving a saint might be easy, but that's not what I'm dealing with.

I don't know that everything will ever be okay. It will be remarkable if things can just be steady for a while. Love is a good starting place, yes. But I don't always feel very loving, especially when I'm the brunt of resistance or even attacks. "Nice" doesn't cut it at times like these. Survival becomes my motivation. I react with power and persistence more than patience. But survival is a facet of love too. Taking a stand for my own well-being tells my loved one that I'm strong and passionate about life and truth and justice. It says that if he'll let in my love rather than fight me, I can bring my strength and passion to bear on his behalf as well.

I'll survive because I care enough to take a stand.

Time for Other Loved Ones

The special care my loved one needs takes a great deal of time and energy. I barely have any left over for the other important people in my life. I feel guilty about shortchanging them. And I feel cheated and even resentful because I don't get to enjoy doing the things I want to do with them.

This guilt and resentment are an added burden. I refuse to be stuck with them. I'm sure there are a few practical changes in my daily routine that would allow me to spend more time with other people I care about. If I can't come up with any on my own, I can brainstorm with others to explore a few options. I can set aside my tendency to say "yes, but" and focus on what might work. Even one change that connects me more with my family or friends can help me feel better. I could at least take a moment to send prayers and thoughts of love to people I love.

I will make one change today to help me enjoy being with someone I love.

Unwelcome Advice

People frequently offer me advice about my loved one's care. Some of it is well-intentioned, but I feel pressured when people say, "What you should do is...." I feel torn. I don't believe anyone knows what I should do. Yet I wonder if I should go ahead and do what's been suggested.

It helps when I remember that I am under no obligation to accept advice. I don't even have to listen to it if it feels more like a burden than a help. If people start to push their opinions on me, I set limits respectfully. I tell them I fully understand their strong feelings and then change the subject. If they're giving advice because they sincerely want to help, I tell them what kind of help I really want. I may ask them to do something fun with me or to take on a task that would lighten my load. If I do want advice, I ask for it and then trust my own wisdom to determine whether it is right for me and my loved one.

I accept or reject the advice of others as I see fit.

What I Tell Myself

I am not very smart. If I were, I wouldn't keep running into the kind of problems I do. Not only that, I am not as helpful to my loved one or as quick at catching on as I should be. I'm not able to get much right.

If I listened to myself talk like this, I'd think my name is "not." I'm "not" this and "not" that. This way of talking about myself is negative. If I keep telling myself I'm not smart or not quick, that's how I'll act. It's true that I sometimes make decisions that don't seem smart later on, but that doesn't mean I'm not smart. I've simply made choices that didn't work out. I could say the same about my other "not" self-descriptions. What I tell myself has power. What if I told myself "I'm smart" or "I'm a quick learner" or "I'm a helpful person"? Like the little engine that thought it could, I'd probably chug along and get to the top more often.

I am capable, smart, caring, and confident.

Help For Depression

My heart aches over my loved one's condition and all that has happened because of it. Sometimes I go numb. I shut down. I get to the edge of depression.

But I don't want to allow myself to be swallowed up by depression. If I did, I wouldn't be any good for my loved one or for me. Once I see that I've lost energy and interest, or see that I have other signs of depression, I'd best grab onto any little trace of strength I can to get some help for myself. It may mean taking medications or seeking nutritional solutions or getting counseling. It may mean getting some rest or getting together with supportive people. It may mean praying or reconnecting with uplifting messages. When I start to think I can't function, a few small steps to take care of myself can get me on the road to recovery.

When depression sets in, I seek help.

Learning

I wish my loved one were able to catch on more easily to what she needs to do to take care of herself. With her condition changing, she has to figure how to do a number of things differently, yet she can't seem to remember what's she told.

Of course, in her condition, it must be hard for her to learn and remember. I'm having a hard enough time myself and I am the well one here. Perhaps she'll never be able to figure out all the new things she needs to know. I may have to be the student for her and stay on as her tutor. This is not a time for her to be learning a lot of new things, it's a time for survival. I'm wasting energy if I fret over her slowness to catch on.

I will learn what is needed to support my loved one.

Advocacy

I want the health care professionals to fully understand my loved one's condition and to give him the best possible treatment and services. It's their job.

This is what I've always expected of doctors—to "fix" people. As a child, I expected them to know what to do when I had a sore throat or sprained ankle—and usually they did know. But my loved one's condition is a lot more complicated. There are no easy or sure fixes for him. Professional helpers can't know everything about his particular condition. In fact, I'm often the one who is most familiar with his symptoms and his reactions to treatments and other services. I would do well to become as educated as I can be about his condition so I can be a good advocate for him. And if his professional caregivers don't have complete information or brush me off when I try to talk with them, I need to have the courage to insist on their cooperation.

*I stay well-informed and well-prepared
to advocate for my loved one.*

Abilities Regained

Moments come along when my loved one is at his best. I get glimpses of how he used to be when he was fully capable. He rises briefly above his present circumstances. I am inspired and touched.

Those moments are comforting. They help me remember all the times when my loved one's abilities seemed limitless. They remind me that he is not gone, only some of his capabilities. In those moments, I feel both nostalgic and hopeful. If I'm not careful, I can get swept up into thinking that he's regaining what he's lost. Of course, in some situations, that may be the case. But for the most part, I simply appreciate the momentary reconnection with those faded aspects of him.

I am grateful for my loved one's abilities,
past and present.

Choosing To Be Here

Why am I taking care of my loved one? Some days I wonder. I didn't exactly choose this, yet I'm stuck with all the consequences.

But I can choose what to do about it today and from here on. If I think of it as something that I'm stuck with, I will always feel like a victim. I'll "blame" others and feel miserable. The truth is, I have a choice every day to be here or not. Of course, there are consequences either way, but it's always my choice. I can choose to give care out of love, compassion, and commitment, or I can be driven by guilt, fear, resignation, and resentment. If I take charge and make a choice, then I bring my whole self into the act. I am steering my life. If I feel resigned about what I'm doing, then events outside me are steering my life. I end up feeling depressed or spending my energy fighting the course I'm on. Making a conscious choice is the more responsible, powerful, and free course to take.

Today I choose to give care to my loved one.

Denial

My loved one isn't always willing to face the truth about her health condition. She denies she has it, or she denies how bad it is and refuses the treatment that's been prescribed. It's painful to watch what happens when her condition deteriorates because she can't or won't accept the truth. Sometimes I just want to shake her and make her see reality.

I know that people often deny their health problems. I don't like it, but that's how it is. I can't force my loved one to accept what she is not ready to accept. I can't make her comply with the treatment regimen if she's not willing. The truth is, I get into denial myself sometimes. I, too, don't want to face this condition and all that it means for my life. Maybe what's called for here is patience and compassion, mixed with occasional firmness, as we both work on coming to terms with her health problems.

I am patient with myself as I let in the truth
a little at a time.

Family Portraits

Family photo albums usually show everyone looking so happy. That's how we think families are supposed to be—smiling, having a good time. But that's not how our faces always look. Sometimes we look solemn and exhausted because we've been through so much.

Whether everyone is smiling or solemn doesn't matter. Our family portrait is a picture full of heart. What counts is whether we are together in spirit. Being family means we stand by each other, care about the smallest details of each other's lives, tell each other the truth when other people won't. We show up for each other in good times and bad. We're not perfect but we have a love that binds us. I'm glad I've got a family to spend time with and take pictures of, whether smiling or not.

I picture my family as all heart.

Feeling Left Out

I don't know what to do when my loved one gets quiet, withdrawn. I understand she needs private time occasionally to just be with her illness, to absorb all it means, to find strength, to face disappointments and despair. But I feel left out, abandoned. I wonder what I've done. I wonder what I can do.

I wish she would tell me why she is being so quiet, but if she doesn't, I try not to take it personally. I let her have the space she needs to deal with things in her own way. I tell her that I will be there for her when she is ready to talk. At the same time, I am compassionate toward myself, tending to my own loss and disappointment when she pulls back. If I cry, it is all right. A friend or my support group can comfort me. Writing in my journal may help. I use this opportunity to take some alone time for myself and sift through all that has been happening.

I respect my loved one's choice to be alone —
and my own sense of loss when she pulls away.

Feeling Depleted

Most people think I'm strong and don't need any help. I do try to keep a positive attitude and avoid feeling sorry for myself. But there comes a time when I'm not so strong, when I'm run down, depleted. At times like that, I want a little tender loving care for myself.

Who do I know with a gentle, caring heart? Maybe I could give her a call and explain how I'm feeling. I could ask if she would spend a little time with me doing something that I enjoy and that gives me energy. Maybe we could watch a comedy together or have a picnic in a quiet spot or visit a gallery or shop I like—anything that wouldn't require a lot of effort on my part. A change of scenery and a little down time would do me good. Having a caring friend nearby will help me feel supported and less alone.

I sustain my energy by asking for support.

Different Strengths

I can take care of some of my loved one's needs easily. But others I fumble with terribly. I'm just not cut out to do some things very well.

Some of the things I have trouble with, other people do with ease. Or at least they don't seem to mind them as much as I do. Maybe it would help if I put most of my energy into the activities I do well and then enlist other people to do what they do well. That way I would be making the most of everyone's strengths. Perhaps I can't hand off everything I do poorly, but even shifting some responsibilities would lighten the pressure on me. Even if I have to pay or barter for some services, it might be worth it if that would diminish my stress and free me to take care of other pressing matters.

I use my strengths and I call on others for theirs.

Embarrassment

Certain things my loved one does embarrass me. His offensive behavior makes me reluctant to invite people over or to go out in public with them. I do what I can to prevent this behavior, but I can only do so much.

Because I feel very close to him, I tend to think that what he does reflects on me. But it helps to remember that I am not responsible for his behavior. I cannot change (or take credit for) his personality or attitudes; and most of his physical and mental problems are out of my control as well. Some of these things he can't change either. What is, is. While people, including myself, may not like everything my loved one does, he is still a precious human being who deserves respect, love, and companionship. I do what I can to help him contain his offensive actions and to retain his dignity when he can't.

I accept my loved one as he is.

Intuition

I am so tuned in to my loved one that at times I instinctively know what's needed before she says anything. I just have a sense about things. I know what I know, even when the evidence is not obvious to others. But I don't catch everything. I'd like to have a stronger intuition.

I know intuition can be developed. Some people say it comes from the "third eye." Some say it comes from the heart. Others claim spiritual inspiration. All I know is that when I quiet my mind a little and open my heart, I have a better chance of sensing what is happening with my loved one. I soften my heart and mind so they open up wide like a spring tulip, and I allow myself to receive information as easily as sunlight. It's a kind of inner knowing. What I discover this way feels as though it comes to me from my soul. I treat it with respect.

I treasure my sense of intuition
and trust what comes to me.

Lack of Appreciation

I do a lot for my loved one but a "thank you" is all too rare. I feel taken for granted. It's not that I don't want to be as helpful as I can, but I'd like to know that what I do is valued.

I realize I can't make other people appreciate me. The feeling has to be genuine on their part. Maybe my loved one and others do appreciate what I do, but they don't show it the way I wish they would. Maybe they're showing it in other ways and I haven't noticed. I could listen for messages from their hearts, even if the words aren't there. I could even ask people directly if they value certain things I do and directly tell them that I'd welcome a word of thanks now and then. In my journal, I could write a thank-you letter to myself, or I could smile at myself in the mirror and tell myself what a good job I'm doing. I don't have to depend on others to find the value in myself.

Who I am and what I contribute are wonderful
and worthy of appreciation.

Mistakes

With so much on my mind, I slip up from time to time. I forget appointments, grab the wrong package, or make a snap decision. There is so much at stake here: What if my error results in a catastrophe? People are depending on me and I don't want to let them down.

I get tense when I worry about making mistakes. I'm on guard, trying to get everything perfect. But that's unrealistic: No one gets everything perfect. It makes sense to be conscientious, but when I make myself tense and fearful I only increase the chances of making mistakes. Maybe it's time to ease the pressure on myself. Maybe I could even learn to laugh at my slip-ups instead of agonizing over them. Most of them are not that serious. If one of my mistakes caused a problem, I would make every effort to correct it, but most are just reminders that I'm human—and that's okay.

When I lighten up, I'm less likely to make mistakes,
or panic when I do.

My Spiritual Power

I know it would help me to have a more active spiritual life, but I'm not sure how to go about that. I've had some experience with religion, but more than ever now, I want to feel a deeper connection to my soul.

One thing I'm sure of: There is some kind of God or other Spiritual Power operating in my life. However I name it, I know I've experienced moments of deep awe that give me a sense of something sacred. If I want more of those moments, then I need to do more of those things that inspire me, give me hope, and convey the deep truths about life. I can adopt religious values that make sense to me, and I can also look inside myself for the ways I experience spiritual strength. I could take a moment today to make a list of the values I hold and the ways I experience a Spiritual Power in my life.

I will get better acquainted with my Spiritual Power today.

Pushing Hard for an Answer

I get furious at the health problem that has made my loved one so debilitated. I want it to go away. I am going to do everything I can to fight this thing. I refuse to let it ruin our lives.

I know that my commitment will help me pursue every possible solution. Sometimes I am more determined to find an answer than my loved one is. I don't want to give up. But maybe I press too hard sometimes. It might help to remember that some things are beyond my control. It's important that I am committed to the best possible outcome, but that may be a different outcome than I'm insisting on now. My intensity and toughness may overshadow the softness I need in order to take in the emotional and spiritual impact of this experience. I may miss the meaning looking for the magic.

I stay open to the best answers wherever I find them.

Reacting

Somebody says something and I react. A criticism, a suggestion, even a comment I don't like sets me off. My blood pressure jumps. I get a headache. I stew and fret. I wish other people wouldn't upset me the way they do.

Of course, no one is forcing me to get upset. When I react, I'm letting other people's actions take over my emotions. I'm giving them the power to make me unhappy and stressed. It's not surprising that, with all the concerns I have about my loved one, I'm prone to letting what others do upset me. But I feel more peaceful when, instead of letting in their comments, I let them go. I just close a door in my mind and say, "No thanks." I turn these thoughts away, just like I turn away an unwelcome salesperson at my door. Nothing personal, just "No thanks."

Today I'll practice saying "No thanks" when I don't like what someone says to me.

Special Needs

Other people don't understand how difficult it is for my loved one. They get impatient with him or dismiss him because they think he's just being difficult. Some people even get jealous of how much attention he gets.

I especially have trouble with family members who refuse to accept and make adjustments for the realities of his condition. I get angry at how selfish they seem. Professional helpers also annoy me when they give up on him or scold him for things he can't help. They should know better. I have so much love for him that I can't stand to see him treated this way. I realize I can't control how other people think. But I encourage professional helpers to treat my loved one with respect and appropriate care. If necessary, I insist they do so. With family members, I practice patience. I try to explain his situation to them and tell them how I'd prefer they treat him.

I respect my loved one's special needs
and I ask others to do the same.

When I've Lost It

Sometimes I just lose it. I get angry and I say things I later wish I hadn't. Once they're out of my mouth, I can't take them back. I feel bad.

I try to make up when I've gotten carried away. I'm extra nice for a while. But I know that doesn't really take the sting out of what I did. What helps more is a direct and sincere apology. That's not always easy. The person I hurt may use my apology as an occasion to bring up more wrongs I've done. But whatever the other person says doesn't change my need to say I'm sorry. If I keep my focus on making a sincere apology, I can listen openly to what the other person says without becoming defensive. I offer to do what is necessary to make things right, but if the other person persists in making negative comments, I don't let that disturb my peace. I simply own what I am responsible for and dismiss the rest.

> *Sincere apologies release my guilt and*
> *help to restore my peace of mind.*

Familiar Places, Familiar Pain

I feel huge resistance sometimes when I go to the hospital or other places where my loved one needs services. I've been in these places before, and they bring up unpleasant memories and fears.

When I notice these feelings, I respect them. It's important to be gentle with myself as I make the decision to support my loved one in places where I have suffered. If I write in my journal or talk with a friend or say a prayer, it's easier to release the old feelings that come back in these painfully familiar settings. What I'm learning is to separate my experiences in the past from my loved one's circumstances in the present. I remind myself that I am not going back to the old problems I had in these places, I am assisting my loved one. I keep the focus on him and his needs. I use this opportunity to create new, more positive memories in these places. I let the love I feel for my dear one take over, fill me with compassion, and renew my sense of hope.

No place can harm me.

Feeling Guilty for What I Have

When my loved one has severe symptoms, I feel so bad for him. And I feel guilty because I'm not suffering the way he is. I can do things he can't do and may never be able to do.

Whenever his symptoms worsen, the contrast becomes sharper. I can see more clearly that he doesn't have the capabilities or freedom I have. I wonder why it has to be this way. I'm left with that question and no real answers. I start to think that somehow I'm responsible, that I shouldn't have it so good when he has it so bad. Of course, my having it good makes no difference to his condition at all. And certainly it would do him no good if somehow I were as miserable as he is. There is no connection. I can enjoy what I have without guilt and without harming him in any way.

Guilt clouds my compassion with too much self-importance.

Love, the Powerhouse

I'm doing things as a caregiver that surprise me. If anyone had asked me earlier how I'd handle some of the challenges that have come up, I couldn't have imagined a solution. But I have indeed figured out how to handle them. I didn't know I had it in me.

I must be more creative than I realized. Yes, creative and resilient and strong. Where did all this capability come from? The answer must be love. I would not have done these things if I had not had so much love for my dear one. It is love that has prompted me to change my whole routine, make hundreds of phone calls and many trips, unravel complicated medical concepts and procedures, persist in getting what was needed, and do many other momentous tasks. I couldn't have done any of this if I didn't care so deeply. What a powerhouse love is! Whenever I am weary or weak, I will remember how love has carried me through.

Love will find a way.

Gentle Care for My Tired Spirit

Sometimes I feel spent. I give and give until I have nothing left to give. I just want to lie down for days. More than that, I want to feel comforted, to be held and cared for.

I know there are friends and other caring people who would help out if they knew how drained I feel. I could ask them for some very special help. It would mean becoming vulnerable and admitting I'm in need of some tender care, but the truth is, I am. I could ask people to come and pray for me, to hold me and let me cry, to sing or read poetry to me, or to give me a backrub. I could ask for something specific or I could just tell them I need a lot of nurturing and let them come up with their own way of tending my languishing spirit and exhausted body.

I allow myself the luxury of being tenderly cared for.

Group Caring

I'm feeling stressed, and so are the other people involved in my loved one's care. His condition—and everything that has resulted from it—have taken a toll on us. We get cross with each other. I know my loved one feels the effects of the tension, too.

It may be time for us to have a talk together. We're all trying so hard, and we may not want to admit how tough this is for us. If we're going to make it through this, we need to find ways to ease the strain we're all experiencing. I'm tempted to tell some of the people that they should change what they're doing. But I know that wouldn't go over very well. Instead, I could be direct and describe the tension I notice and suggest that we talk about ways to alleviate it. Perhaps we could take turns asking for one thing that would make the situation easier for each of us. Or we could tell what we're most worried about or feel the saddest about.

We can care for each other while caring
for our loved one.

Learning New Skills

I don't know if I can do all the things that are required of me as a caregiver. I was never trained for this. I'm constantly being asked to do things I thought were only done by medical professionals. I'm not prepared.

Learning all these things takes tremendous patience. I don't always get it right. I guess that's not surprising since this is all so new to me. Mistakes are a part of any learning process. I didn't learn to ride a bike or drive a car on my first attempt. I don't want to be too hard on myself, just as I wouldn't yell at a child trying to learn math. It takes time to learn. Slowing down makes it easier when I'm trying something new. If I'm having trouble catching on, I can ask for more help and instruction from the professionals until I develop adequate skills and confidence. If I remember I'm a beginner, I'll give myself all the time I need.

*I am learning the best I can, at the rate
that's best for me.*

Magnificent Moments

There are moments when I am thrilled for my loved one. Despite all the agony he suffers and restrictions he lives with, he pulls off some amazing feats. I am so happy for him.

My heart nearly explodes with pride as I watch him go way beyond what appear to be his limits. He seems powered at the moment by an extra burst of courage or love and I feel compelled to do everything I can to assist him. It's almost as if something bigger than both of us takes over and we ride together on a high. I feel like I'm supporting a champion, and I too go beyond my limits. I'm so glad we have moments like these. In days when we're having lots of difficulties, I remind him—and myself—of how magnificent these special times were. They reawaken a feeling of courage and love in both of us when we desperately need it.

My loved one is a magnificent being and so am I.

People Who Seem to Care

I am annoyed when certain people become overly friendly after hearing about my loved one's condition. These people usually ignore me or are mean to me. Now they seem to be treating me nice because they feel sorry for me.

Funny how everything seems to get on my nerves these days—even people being nice to me. Maybe it's because I'm so angry about having to deal with this situation that I have a hard time trusting other people's intentions. But it's not fair to assume others have bad intentions. Maybe they've had a genuine change of heart. Other folks' problems have a way of bringing out the best in people. This may be a time to weigh in my heart whether I want to be open to their concern or whether I would do best to avoid them for now. Either way I know I am worthy of genuine care.

*I surround myself with people who care
from the heart.*

Loss and Regeneration

When I look ahead, I get discouraged sometimes. The long-term picture for my loved one doesn't look good. I try to keep my hopes up, but I see the future as a series of losses. I get sad.

To comfort myself, I turn to nature. Loss is everywhere—animals shedding fur and skin, trees dropping their fruit, stones and seashores wearing away from the constant washing of the waters. Nature is also filled with new life and beauty coming forth on the tail of losses—a butterfly emerging from a shed cocoon, a lively newborn leaving behind an empty womb, a vibrant spring budding after winter dormancy. Loss and regeneration are nature's rhythm. I can trust this is right.

I bear with the losses and await the birth
of new things.

No Debts to Repay

I owe my loved one so much. I have received so many gifts from her over the years, and now I'm getting a chance to pay back a debt.

Of course, I can never really pay back what I received from her. That was never the idea in the first place. What my loved one gave me was indeed a gift; no payback was expected or needed. If I try to repay a debt, my giving to her might start to feel like an obligation rather than an expression of genuine love. I don't really "owe" anything, but I am free to express the same kind of generous care I received from my loved one, and I am glad I am able to do it. At the same time, I honor and appreciate all that she has given to me.

I give my love and care freely to my loved one.

Problems or Adventures?

No matter how carefully laid out my plans, something always comes up to change them. My loved one takes a turn for the worse. A service provider doesn't come through. I get sick. Just once I'd like things to work out as planned.

Of course, they do work out much of the time. I only notice them more when they don't. Life wouldn't be life if our plans were guaranteed. Part of the fun of living is that surprises keep coming up. I can look at them as problems or as adventures: real "action adventures." What twists and turns will this story take? What will the hero or heroine do to outfox the "bad guy"? In this case, I get to cast myself as the "good guy." I get to be as creative or bold or foxy as I want to be. If I decide to have some fun with the interruptions, it may turn out that my original plan wasn't nearly as interesting or effective as the actual end result.

When I make plans, I expect to find
some surprise adventures in the plot.

Listening with Attention

I like to solve problems. So when my loved one brings me her troubles, my mind begins racing in search of solutions. But as I scan my brain for ideas, I'm only half listening to her and I miss some of what she says.

I realize that genuine listening calls for complete attention. In my rush to find answers, I actually create distance between us. My mind leaves the conversation to seek the quickest possible fix. I start to analyze the information she gives me, picking and choosing what I hear to fit a specific type of solution. In the process, I miss not only some of what she says, *I miss my encounter with her.* How much more effective I am when I let her storytelling go where it goes. She's in the midst of a discovery process and I am a witness. I respect the journey she's on, even when she detours or stops to rest. I allow room for solutions to emerge in their own good time.

My loved one has stories to tell and I listen.

Trusting Others

When I have to depend on so many people to take part in my loved one's care, I feel insecure. I don't know if I can trust them and I don't always like how they do things. I'd rather just do it all myself so I can be in control.

Of course, I can't do everything myself. I need others with the time and skills I don't have to help with his care. But I get frightened that they'll make my loved one uncomfortable or fail to give him what he needs. Yet I can't be there to control all that happens. And my worrying about the situation doesn't help anyone, of course. Once I've done what I can to ensure that he has reasonably competent and caring caregivers, then I would be wise to relax and let them do their job. If it isn't exactly the way I would do it, that's okay. There are many good ways to get things done.

> *I trust that others will give good care*
> *to my loved one.*

When I'm Sick

I don't always feel well. When I have a headache or catch one of the "bugs" going around, I feel like turning in my resignation as a caregiver. I want to rest. I want to be left alone.

One thing I can do when I'm sick is to ease up and let some nonessential things go until I feel better. I can also try to get someone else to fill in for me so I can take time to rest and recover. I don't have to be a hero. I can let the person I'm caring for know that I can't handle everything today and ask for understanding. If I find I'm acting impatiently when I feel ill, I will recognize my impatience as a signal I need some relief. I'll look for ways to be kind to myself so I can regain my health and my patience.

I treat myself well when I'm sick.

Time for Others

Too often I find myself apologizing to people because I can't do something with them or for them. My responsibilities to my loved one limit what I can do otherwise. But I feel like I should be more involved with others, and I wish I could be.

For now, I am choosing to spend a significant amount of my time caring for my loved one. As I am able, I make plans to do a few things I enjoy with others. If people ask more of me than I am able or willing to give right now, I don't need to apologize for saying no. I can honestly admit to myself and to others that I'd like to be doing more, but it's not my responsibility to do something just because others ask.

I am in charge of my own time.

Resistance

I don't understand why my loved one doesn't always go along with what I've arranged for her. When I've figured out what's obviously the best for her and gone through all the effort to set things up, you'd think she'd be grateful and cooperate.

However, I tend to forget sometimes what an adjustment it is for her to go through so many changes. Even when it's in her best interest, even when she can't decide and I have to, it is still tough for her to accept decisions she hasn't been able to make for herself. I do my best to make choices that will best suit her situation, but they are still my choices. She has to live with them. I am learning to be patient with her as she learns to let go of the control she no longer has. I give her room for resistance. To the extent I can, I check out her preferences and honor them. If she is argumentative, I don't take it personally. I do all I can to ease the adjustments she has to make.

I insist when necessary, but I do so with love.

Staying in Balance

I've heard the old sayings many times: You should be grateful—after all, things could be worse. Stop feeling sorry for yourself. You've got to toughen up.

There is some truth to those old sayings. I am glad things are not worse than they are. And self-pity will do me no good. But it's also true that I've got my hands full with these caregiving responsibilities and at times, that seems like too much to bear. I want to be honest about that. I don't want to exaggerate my problems, but I don't want to minimize them either. Facing my situation honestly keeps me in balance. It helps me toughen up when I need to and ease up on myself when I need some relief.

I stay in balance by being honest and realistic about my circumstances.

Hearing about a Death

Whenever I hear about the death of someone who had the same health condition as my loved one, a wave of fear rolls through me. I don't want to hear about it. Yet I find myself listening for the details to see how closely they match my loved one's situation.

I don't want my loved one to die. Yet sometimes I think death would be for the best if her suffering gets to be too much; it's comforting to think she'll be free from her agony. But I can't deny I'm afraid of the pain that goes with losing someone so precious to me. Losing her will rip away at the deep bond we have and my heart will bleed and her death will remind me of my own destiny someday. I want to keep death away, but I can't. In thinking about death, it helps if I remember what happens when seeds are buried in the soil. They lose their current form entirely and yet they give rise to daisies or corn stalks or mulberry trees. I let nature take me through its paces.

I fear death, yet I respect its mysteries.

Mischief and Make-believe

The craziness, the chaos, the paradox surrounding my loved one's situation get to be too much some days. I can't make much sense of anything and I start to lose it. I can't believe things are happening the way they are.

When things get goofy beyond belief, it's time to stop believing and get goofy. Few events are so serious that I can't poke fun at them. A little bit of mischief may be what will save my sanity. A piece of ribbon can become a Charlie Chaplin bow tie. A plastic bowl can become a hat. A pillow case over my head or a large bandage across my face can become a bandit costume. Converting a sock into a puppet and staging a "drama" can flatten a mountain of tension. A litany of puns can make my day. Where does it say I can't laugh when life is too bizarre to take seriously?

A little bit of mischief gets me through the madness.

Loss of Favorite Activities

My caregiving responsibilities keep me so busy that I don't get to do some of the things I like to do. I really miss them. I feel angry and disappointed. I suppose I shouldn't feel that way. My loved one has had to give up so much more than I have.

Still, I've had many losses since I began caregiving. This is one more. Yes, my loved one has lost a lot, but that doesn't diminish my own sense of missing what's been important to me. Any loss, no matter what kind or size, can be significant. I don't want to downplay what I'm going through. I want to be conscious of my experiences and appreciate both the pain and the blessing of each one. I want to cherish the memories of activities I've enjoyed and anticipate doing them again some day. I want to respect the grief and anger and disappointment I feel and find a helpful way to express those feelings. Then I can more easily let go of these activities and be present to what is in front of me.

I mourn and release the activities I cannot do now.

Detachment

One person in my family gets to me. When it's her turn to show up and help out, something "comes up" and she expects me to step in. Or else she takes over completely. I get so angry. I wish she would cooperate.

But I know the way we interact won't change unless I decide to make a change. The first thing I need to do is to work on detaching my emotions from her behavior—to "not care." As part of not caring, I avoid judging her as right or wrong. That's suddenly not important if I don't care. Detaching takes a while to get used to, but I get better with practice. When she wants to back out of helping, for example, I simply let her know, without hostility or judgment, that I won't step in. I stand firm despite her pleas and I leave it to her to figure out what to do. One little change like that starts to "unhook" me from constant fretting about her behavior. When I focus on my own actions, I feel more peaceful.

One change changes the relationship.

A Stranger

My loved one seems like a stranger sometimes. So much has changed that it seems like I'm caring for someone I hardly know. I wish I could have back the person I remember.

The changes have been drastic. My foundations have been shaken. It is not the same anymore. It never will be and the sadness almost swallows me up at times. What is asked of me now is a new level of love for this person who has been so special in my life. It's a stretch—some days a big stretch—but I know the love is there and it will carry me through. I am patient with myself as I learn to meet these big changes and tap into this deeper love. I don't chide myself for my feelings of resistance; they are normal and honest. I write them down or share them with an understanding friend or with my Spiritual Power. That helps diffuse them and make room for the love.

*I accept my feelings of resistance
and give them a voice.*

Accidents

Because my loved one has limited abilities, things get dropped, spilled, broken. Then I have to clean them up. Sometimes I just want to do everything myself to keep accidents from happening.

I know it's not his fault. He doesn't mean to make a mess. But I'm caught between my compassion for him and my frustration at the disasters that are created. Well, maybe "disasters" is an exaggeration. Most of the time, cleaning up the mess takes just a few minutes, and there is no serious damage. The real "mess" is inside me, because I'm so stressed by the demands of caregiving that any little accident feels like the last straw. It might help if I paid better attention to my own stress level. My overreaction to an accident might be a helpful clue that it's time for me to show some compassion toward myself. It could prompt me to find some ways to slow down and lighten my load. Then I could more easily keep minor messes in perspective.

Accidents happen.

Closed Heart

Sometimes I am overwhelmed from giving so much time and attention to my loved one. It takes too much out of me. I can't afford to care that much anymore. Something in me decides that I'll do only what I need to do and block out my feelings.

My heart closes. Numbness takes over and I go on automatic. But in doing that, I give up a core piece of myself. I become a dutiful robot. This is too great a price to pay. I want to open my heart again. I could start by comforting my tense and weary body. As a baby, when I got tense or frantic, I was soothed by rocking. I could do that for myself now. A rocking chair might do the trick, or I can just rock myself a little wherever I'm sitting. Or I could lie on the floor, and with my heels staying in place, I could extend and flex my feet, rocking my whole body with them for a time. Rocking has a softening effect. It restores an even rhythm and helps my caring come back into balance.

Rocking reassures my careworn heart.

Eating Well

I find it hard to eat right. Sometimes I eat constantly just to pass the time or to get the good feeling that food gives me. Other times I don't bother to eat or I just eat junk. My body feels the effects. I'm sluggish and my digestion is poor.

My body needs good care. I need to be healthy if I'm going to have the energy to keep giving care to my loved one. I want to be healthy, for my own sake as well as hers. The junk food has got to go, at least most of it. It helps when I take a minute or two each morning to think ahead and plan specifically how to get the well-balanced meals I want and need during that day. Anytime I start to reach for junk food or more food than I need, I ask myself whether the hunger I feel is for food or for something else. When I'm tempted to skip a meal, I remind myself of my need for regular nourishment.

I respect my body by eating food that nourishes me.

Distracted

I drop things. I miss half of what someone says. I lose track of things I need. I get so distracted, I wonder if I've lost my mind. I'm sure it's because I've got a lot to keep track of, but still, I get disturbed when so many important things slip by me.

Distraction is just what the word suggests—being "off track." Maybe just realizing I'm distracted is a good reminder to get myself back "on track." If I'm not tuning in to what's going on around me, it's because my attention is somewhere else. Nothing is more important than this moment because it is the only real moment I have to live. I might need to slow down for a bit to bring my attention here so I can fully take in what's in front of me. If my mind is racing ahead or is caught up in the swirl of what happened an hour ago, I won't be able to absorb what this moment has to offer. A pause, a deep breath, and a choice to focus bring me back to the moment, back to myself.

The opposite of distraction is intentional presence.

I've Come This Far

I didn't think I could do this at first. When my loved one's health problems first appeared, and then all the complications came about, I was overwhelmed. So much to learn! So many barriers to overcome!

It's amazing how well I've managed. What I didn't know how to do, I've been learning. I've managed to chip away at what seemed like impossible barriers. I've found resources and made arrangements as needed. I've taken a firm stand when necessary. People have stepped in to help. I don't exactly have everything under control, but I'm handling a lot of things reasonably well. Day by day, I'm gaining confidence that I will be able to manage each new thing that comes up.

I'm getting through this one day at a time.

Getting out of "Jail"

I feel like I'm in jail. I'm having to do things I never thought I'd have to and I don't like it. It's hard enough to do them once, but the thought of having to do them for weeks or months or years is almost more than I can bear some days.

One way people in jail keep from going crazy is by letting free their imagination. My mind is not in jail. I can keep my thoughts on pleasant things—on cherished memories or on dreams, even fantasies. I can be a "jailbreaker" in my mind and have fun with wild and playful and inventive ideas. My imagination can even transform what's in front of me: the wheelchair can become a personal water-craft, the medicine bottle can turn into Aladdin's lamp.

My imagination is unlimited and I'm free to soar.

Lost in Caregiving

My life is filled with caregiving responsibilities. I schedule my whole day around them. I've lost touch with many of the people and activities that used to interest me.

Oddly, I've come to depend on caregiving as my way of life. I've lost myself in it. I'm doing it for a good reason, of course; I love my dear one. But I want my caregiving to be an extension of myself, not the other way around. I'd like the care I give my loved one to be part of the bigger circle of caring I'm involved in. My circle seems small now, but could it grow? What else beyond caregiving could I include in my circle? What interests or people or activities do I care about besides my loved one? How can I branch out to take them back into my life? When I picture caregiving as just one of the activities I include in my circle, I am putting myself back where I belong—in the middle of the circle, extending myself outward.

I keep caregiving as only one facet of my identity.

My Capabilities

My loved one can't do some of the simplest things I take for granted. I could give a long list of "normal" activities that he can't manage now and never will be able to do. I don't know if I always appreciated before how hard it is to lose those little daily living skills.

I get teary-eyed when I think of what he's not able to do. His lost abilities are also a wake-up call for me. They make me appreciate what I can do. I have hands and feet and eyes and ears and a mind and senses that work. I am free to move about, take care of my daily needs, and interact with the world without making a huge effort or seeming like a misfit. When I realize that I may not have these capabilities forever, I am prompted to take full advantage of them. I take good care of my body to keep it working well and I enjoy pursuing my interests while I can.

I love my body and enjoy what it allows me to do.

Not Enough Sleep

I know I don't get enough sleep. I don't have time to sleep as much as I should. And my loved one's needs sometimes require me to get up during the night. Then I have trouble getting back to sleep. I can't keep going on like this.

I wonder what I could do to build a little more sleep into my schedule. I may need to arrange for respite care or other assistance to give me time to sleep. It might help to stop whatever I'm doing at a set time each night and go to bed. A soothing ritual before bedtime might help me get to sleep. I certainly need to avoid caffeine, alcohol, and other stimulants before going to bed. If worries keep me awake, saying a surrender prayer or pushing an imaginary "pause" button could help. Taking a half dozen slow, deep, relaxing breaths or doing other relaxation exercises might relieve tension that keeps me awake.

I value my sleep and I take steps
to make sure I get enough.

Asking Permission

I've learned about some special ways of healing that I'm quite sure would help my loved one. I don't know if she will agree to use them. I wonder how to convince her.

Of course, I always want to respect her personal boundaries in whatever I do. If she can make decisions herself, it's important that I get her permission before doing anything to her. If she is incapable of making a choice, I can seek the permission of her soul. While I may have a good idea for helping her, she has a right to determine what she is willing to experience. If I invade her boundaries by doing things that are out of sync with her sensibilities, I am not offering healing. I'm diverting her from her own journey toward wholeness. But when I have her permission, I can work in harmony with her and healing is more likely.

I ask permission out of respect
for my loved one's own desires.

Renewable Energy

I've run out of gas. It's like stepping on a car starter and there's no juice. I feel so empty I can hardly move my hands and feet, let alone think a clear thought. Yet my loved one needs more from me, and I have many things of my own to do.

Maybe it's time to stop for a "fill-up." To replenish myself, I can draw up the wonderful energy of the earth that sustains the plants and draw in the life-giving energy of the sun. First, I quiet myself and let my empty spaces open. I allow myself to sense the earth's renewing energy seeping in through the bottom of my feet. It moves very slowly up my legs, into my torso, and all the way up to my heart. With each breath, more energy fills my body. Then I imagine the sun's energy pouring in through the top of my head until it meets the earth energy and mixes with it. I feel tingly and alive and my body is renewed.

I am open to giving my energy
and to being replenished.

Worry about Money

I worry a lot about money. I don't know how I will manage. The bills keep piling up, and they're all so confusing. I don't how to get them all straightened out and paid.

One thing I know for sure is that worry won't pay any bills. It only makes me feel worse. What I can do is to get my finances organized and make necessary decisions. I look at one bill at a time and then make any phone calls or write out a check or take other actions to make sure it gets handled. I do the same with the rest of the bills and with other financial paperwork, one item at a time. Between working on each one, I stop and take a breather to keep from feeling too stressed; but then I continue until I get caught up. If I can't manage by myself I can ask someone to help me. My worry is all about fear. If I get busy working on solutions, my fear will get smaller.

Today I'll move from worry into action.

Expanded Vision

I have a limited number of options when it comes to providing care for my loved one. I can only afford so much. The services available are limited. I've only got so much time. Considering what we have to work with, I don't see how to make things better even though I'd like to.

I know some of the limits are just the limits of my own vision. It's as though I have one eye covered and don't have a full view. If I can contact organizations or individuals who can give me more information, I may find more options. Perhaps I can ask someone to brainstorm with me to help me come up with new ideas. Maybe I can create a picture in my mind of what the ideal situation would look like and then make at least some adjustments in my schedule or my spending to move in that direction. There is almost always more than one way to move if I'm willing to open both eyes and look around.

What I am willing to see is what I get.

Family Unity

Anytime my loved one's condition changes, the whole family is affected. Everyone is concerned. We have lots of questions, and some disagreements, about what to do.

An informal family meeting might help us decide how to handle the changes taking place. If some members can't come, we can use a speaker phone or a conference call or some other way to include them. Some members could do research before we meet so we have good information to work with. We could ask a friend or clergy member to lead the meeting, or a wise and respected elder in the family might take the lead. Setting ground rules, such as having mutual respect and staying open-minded, might help. We can allow time for all to express their feelings, but we also need to move toward agreement on some practical steps. While I can't control how others in the family react in such a meeting, I can do my best to participate with love.

Family unity and support ensure the best decisions.

I've Hurt People

I'm not proud of some things I've done as a caregiver. I've been impatient and critical. I've failed to deliver on promises. I've been demanding and sneaky. I don't like admitting these things. I feel ashamed.

They say confession is good for the soul. I suppose it is. While the truth can hurt, facing the truth hurts less than living a lie. When I can admit to myself and to an understanding listener the ways I have caused pain, the burden of those actions gets a little lighter. At first, though, I feel terrible. I tend to judge myself harshly. But then I remember that what I've done is past, and I'm willing to learn to do things in less hurtful ways. I forgive myself, and where necessary, I tell those I've hurt what I'll do to change things for the better. What's most important is to remember that I'm a good person even if I've made some missteps.

I am honest about what I have done
and willing to leave the past behind.

Embarrassed by My Weakness

I want to be loving, in control, and courageous for my loved one; yet all too often I am selfish, fearful, and out of control. When I see that I've fallen short of my ideals, I get embarrassed and uneasy. I get angry at myself.

In those painful moments when I recognize my weaknesses, I don't like what I see. I feel vulnerable—unable to protect myself from the eyes of others. My defenses go down. I don't think well of myself at those times, but I resist trying to cover up my shortcomings and how I feel about them. These are times for genuine honesty. I'm often surprised to find that people are more at ease with me when I'm in this frame of mind. My honesty and vulnerability allow them to acknowledge their own struggles with fear and weakness. And I'm more available to be with them. It's funny how honesty is so healing.

My weaknesses, when owned, harbor strength and safety for others.

Silence Together

I don't know what to say when my loved one is suffering so much. I want to offer a bit of wisdom or reassurance or humor, but nothing seems to fit. My words fall flat. I find myself talking just for the sake of talking, thinking that my words will somehow alleviate the situation.

My words do make a difference at times, but there are other times for silence. If my words are not working, it may be best to stop using them. Just being with my loved one is enough. My silent presence is the gift I can give. No words are necessary. What is created in the silence is room for our two souls to rest together and contemplate. We have a sacred time to be in each other's presence without expectation. If there is anything to communicate, love is the language spoken.

I savor the sweetness of silence with my loved one.

Singing

When the rough times hit, I know I have to do something to keep from going nuts. When everything seems out of control and I am stuck waiting for other people to come through with decisions or resources, I can't just sit around moping or seething. I need something to keep me going and I don't want to turn to food or drugs to numb me.

I could sing. I may not exactly feel like it at first, but give me a recording of a favorite artist and that may be all it takes. I can lip sync or break out into a full-throated solo if no one's around who minds. I don't need to know the words. I can pretend I'm singing in Italian or Japanese. Or I can make up my own lyrics. Even the melody can be an original. Whatever my mood, I can find a tune to tell the world about it.

> *I'll find a song and sing along,*
> *and nothing will bother me.*

Tenuous Life

The life of my loved one is so tenuous. When I gaze at him, I see how fragile he is, how thin the thread between life and death. He has been strong and now he's not. He has lost abilities and is dependent on others. Still, he has life and that life is precious.

I am on holy ground when I stand with him. He reminds me of my connection with a universal sense of being. His life, like mine, has been given; and at some point it will be gone, at least in this form. In this moment of stopping to notice, I don't take life for granted for either of us. I can never be certain at any moment how long either of us will be here. I want to treasure every memory, every experience, every dream that has made up our lives. I want to hang on to them all, but all I have is this moment. He is here and I am here. There is only what we are in this moment, and it is holy.

Life is a gift to be cherished now.

Wanting Control

No one understands as well as I do what my loved one needs. If I'm away for a day, or even a few minutes, it seems that somebody screws something up. I'd like to take a break, but how can I when I'm the only one who can get things done right?

I have to laugh at myself sometimes when I realize how much I want to be in control. I'm so sure I'm right! I'm like a sergeant, giving orders and making sure things get done. But when I think I have to take command like that, I never get to let up. I end up tense and tired a lot. Of course it's just possible that other people who are helping with my loved one's care are also smart and thoughtful people. They may do things in ways I wouldn't, but that doesn't make them wrong. They make mistakes, but so do I, and they're usually not that serious. Maybe I could give others some slack and give myself a breather.

I ease up on the controls and appreciate what others have to offer, even if it's not done my way.

Knowing Myself Better

I thought I knew my limits. I thought I was a pretty kind person. I thought I knew some things for sure. Since dealing with my loved one's condition, most everything I thought I knew has become less of a sure thing.

I'm getting a new picture of who I am. I've seen more of the worst side of myself during these times than I cared to. I've also seen myself go far beyond what I thought I was capable of. It's been humbling and surprising. One of the hardest things has been to give up believing in some of the things I was so sure of when this all started. It's not easy admitting that I was mistaken. Yet, because of all the mistakes and failures and pressures I've lived through, I know myself a lot better than I used to. I've now got more to draw on and less to hide.

I'm glad to be at home with myself.

Kind People

Many people have been kind to me since I've been caregiving. Some of the professional helpers have gone out of their way to give extra help. Friends have shown concern. Other people have offered to step in and help. Sometimes just a caring look or touch or a door being opened for me gives me a sense of being cared about and gets me through the day.

I wonder if people know how much their thoughtful actions mean to me? I don't always have the energy to respond in kind, but I know it's okay to just accept the kindness of others without feeling obligated. Allowing others to give to me is also a gift to them. Of course, I can express appreciation to them, and I can pass the gift of kindness along to someone else. Kindness tends to generate kindness. But some days it's enough just to take it in and be grateful.

> *Today I will enjoy the kindness of others*
> *and breathe a prayer of thanks.*

Intentions

My intentions are good. I mean well when I do things as a caregiver and yet I can't say they always turn out well. Sometimes I innocently misread a situation. Other times I get off to a good start but become too exhausted, distracted, or distraught to follow through. I know I can't go back and change how things have turned out, but I feel bad about them.

Indeed, I can't change the past and I don't want to carry it forward with me. It's old news. My intentions for today are what deserve my attention now. I check to see if they are in alignment with my values, my resources, and the needs of the situation. If so, I move forward confidently. Periodically during the day, I check inwardly to see if I'm on track with my intentions. If not, the check-in reminds me to get back on course. If, despite my best intentions, something doesn't work out exactly as planned, I make adjustments and move forward again.

I live my life intentionally.

Nice Days

People say so casually, "Have a nice day." But there is nothing nice about all too many of my days. I have one unpleasant task to do after another. My loved one suffers, I suffer, and I don't remember what "nice" feels like.

When was the last time I had a nice day? It might do me good to write in my journal about that experience. If I describe in detail everything that made the day so nice, maybe I can recreate the good feelings I was having. I could write about any number of nice days. I've had plenty in my life. It's true that recent times have been rough on me, but I have a history of making the best of difficult circumstances. So I know how to make a day nice even when it may not appear to be. I've been triumphant despite everything being stacked against me. Those victories always felt nice. It will help if I write about them.

Memories of nice days help create a nicer today.

My Work Life

People at work don't understand what I'm dealing with outside of work hours. When I have to take personal phone calls, when I have to leave early, when I can't attend a special after-hours meeting, they think I'm trying to get out of work. It's not true.

I know that right now it's important for me to give my primary attention to my loved one. I don't neglect my work, but I can't always give it my best at this time. I tell my co-workers about my situation if I think it will help me, but I can't expect them to fully understand the demands on my personal life. If they are critical of me, I don't waste a lot of energy defending myself. I do make necessary arrangements to see that my responsibilities are handled and to keep my boss up to speed on my situation. I don't have to feel guilty about slowing down a little at work for a time. I know that when my personal situation stabilizes or improves, I will be able to give a hundred percent at work again.

I keep my work life and personal life in balance.

Comparisons

I've met people who seem to manage caregiving remarkably well. They keep their spirits high, they juggle their many responsibilities with ease, and they don't appear to get tired. I don't know how they do it. I berate myself because I'm not as good as they are.

But that doesn't help. I only feel worse. It's true, I will never respond to caregiving in the same way others do, because I'm not them. I don't have their history, their set of circumstances, their resources. I am me, not them. What matters is not how I compare to them, but rather making choices that work best for me. I learn from others, but I avoid judging myself next to them. If I do notice myself being self-critical, I remind myself how damaging that is to me. Instead I turn my attention to how well I'm doing in my own way. My challenges and strengths are unique and I work with them the best I can.

I appreciate what others do and what I do,
each in our own way.

Craving for Beauty

Ill health isn't attractive. Some of the hands-on things I have to do for my loved one are decidedly unappealing. The mundane, difficult, and even ugly chores I must do can make my day gray in a hurry. I almost forget what beauty is.

It helps to have flowers around and other pretty things. Anything from a colorful calendar photo to a decorative pillow can brighten up a room and bless my eyes. Occasionally, I like to spend a few hours at a gallery or in a garden, or looking at a seed catalog or watching clouds. Even taking a moment when I'm cooking to notice the radiant red of a tomato or the shine on a kernel of corn can satisfy my craving for beauty. Sometimes I stop and look into the eyes of the person I care for, and I find beauty there as well. I can almost see through to the soul.

Everything has a beauty to it if only I stop to look.

Maybe

I keep doubting myself: Maybe I should set up a different schedule. Maybe this isn't the right place for my loved one. Maybe somebody else would know better what to do.

When I waver back and forth like this, I wear myself out. Nothing is ever settled. I'm constantly shifting gears. It helps if I remember that there are no right answers. There are only decisions, and then actions based on those decisions, and then consequences. So when I make a decision, the maybes are over. It's time to rest from the decision and stop the wavering. With the decision complete, I focus my attention on the action and move forward with it. When the action is complete, I experience the consequences, and attend to them. I am fully present to each part of the process, and when each is done, I leave it behind. No more maybes. No more second-guessing.

> *I do what I do, with my whole heart*
> *and my whole mind.*

Messages to Deliver

I have some things I'd like to say to my loved one. They are sensitive in nature, and I'm reluctant to say them. I don't know quite how to say them, and it never seems to be the right time. But they're important. I won't rest easy until I get them said.

I know people who lost their loved ones before they said the things they wanted to say. Their messages were never delivered, and their issues were never settled. I don't want that to happen to me. It's my fear holding me back: I'm afraid I'll be misunderstood or my message will be rejected. But I can't control that. What I can do is to drop my expectations and let the truth do what it does. If I am feeling eager to say something, that's a sign the message is ready for delivery. If I need support, I can ask for encouragement and a chance to practice with a friend. It's time to let the message out.

Today I'll notice my undelivered messages that are ready to take flight and set them free.

No Advice

Almost every time my loved one has a problem, I could offer him some advice. It's also easy for me to tell the other people involved in his care how to handle things better. But people don't always listen to me.

Perhaps I'm too eager with my advice. That's especially true if I thrust it on people, whether they want it or not. It helps if I remember that advice is a gift, but only if it's given in a respectful way, and only if it's wanted. I know I resent it if people give me advice when what I really want is a dose of compassion or a sounding board for my ideas. Advice interrupts my own process of clarification and problem-solving. It also suggests to me that I'm not capable of thinking for myself. I prefer to have people ask me if I want advice before giving it, and it makes sense for me to treat others the same way. If they say no, then it's important that I respect their choice.

My answers are my answers;
others have answers that suit them.

Outbursts

Some days my loved one exhibits a Jekyll-and-Hyde personality. He's cross and even hostile, then he's calm and pleasant. I feel jerked around, confused, and angry.

What I tend to forget is that changes in his physical condition can play a big part in how he reacts to things. Maybe low blood sugar or a medication side effect or lingering brain damage is triggering his behavior. If I watch the patterns of his reactions over time, I can start to tell what's at work in any given situation. I may even be able to help him notice that his body is craving certain nutrients or that he needs a medication change. It helps if I don't take his reactions personally. Of course, insofar as he is able, I expect him to keep these extreme behaviors under control. But when he can't, I dismiss them as passing thunderstorms and look for the sunshine.

I blow off any outbursts that my loved one can't control.

Being Away

Whenever I spend time away from my loved one, I'm on edge. I wonder if everything is all right. I think of things I should have done. If the phone rings, I expect it to be an emergency call. I rarely relax.

When I'm away, it's because I want to be doing something elsewhere. So it would make sense to give that activity my full attention. But instead, I tend to think that if I were back with my loved one, I'd be able to keep things under control and prevent any problems there. But the truth is, even if I were there, a lot of what happened would still be out of my control. Being away is an act of trust. I leave my loved one in others' hands. If I get worried, I stop a moment, release my worries to my Spiritual Power, and return my attention to the activities I've chosen. Whatever happens while I'm away, I can deal with it when I return.

When I choose to be away from my loved one,
I trust that all is well.

Boundaries

My loved one could be doing a number of things that would help him feel better and function better. He could improve his diet, follow his doctor's orders, go to a support group. I try to get him to take better care of himself but without much success.

While I want my loved one to improve, I can't make the changes for him. He has to make those choices for himself. I'm not in charge of his thoughts, feelings, or behavior, and I intrude on him when I try to be. I can ask if he wants my opinion and offer my support, but I can't insist he do things, even if they are good for him. It's important to respect his boundaries, just as I want him to respect mine. If I am frustrated by his lack of self-care, I tell him that, but I don't pout or treat him harshly if he doesn't do what I think he should. My role is not to be judge and punisher. More appropriate for me is to tend to the changes I can make to promote my peace of mind.

My own choices are enough for me to handle.

Discomfort with Body Care

I want to help care for my loved one, but I feel so uncomfortable when I must take care of his personal hygiene. It puts me in a whole different role than I'm used to. I try to be as respectful as possible, but I feel awkward.

I never expected I'd have to care for my loved one this way. It calls for a high degree of love and grace to pull this off. It's hard to admit how hesitant I feel to do these things. I don't want him to think I don't care. But the feelings of embarrassment and even disgust are real; I don't have to be ashamed of them, they're normal. It might ease my feelings if I wrote in my journal about them or confided in someone I trust. It might also help if I could view the care I'm giving in a different light. Perhaps I could think of treating my loved one with the same tenderness and regard that I would give a baby who needs my care.

*I respect my feelings as I learn to provide care
in new ways.*

Good Friends

I don't know how I could manage without my friends. Those who have stayed with me through all the difficulties are treasures. They give me a shoulder to cry on, they offer to help, they lift my spirits. Sometimes I think I don't deserve all that my friends do for me.

I'm so glad I've got the friends I have. I think I'll make a call today to someone who's helped me out. It's also good to keep in mind that friendship takes two people. I'm not only receiving from my friends, I'm also giving my friends some gifts during this time. I am being honest with them by sharing with them my deepest struggles and joys and by welcoming their love and kindness. I have also given a great deal to my friends at other times when they have needed help. Friendship is like that: There is giving and receiving both ways, not because it's deserved, but because of love.

*I'm grateful I have good friends
and that I am a good friend, too.*

Trusting My Decisions

I've had to make many difficult decisions as a caregiver. Some haven't turned out the way I hoped, but most of them have worked out all right. When I started all this, I didn't know if I'd be able to figure out all the things I needed to, but I've done okay.

It's a good feeling to know I can trust myself to make good decisions. I have the ability to gather information and get advice if I need it. I can think through all the possible consequences for everyone affected and then make the decisions that need to be made. I know that no decision is going to bring perfect results. Sometimes the consequences will be unpleasant. But that doesn't make my decision wrong. It is the best decision I could make at the time. Whatever the consequences, the next step is simply to make a decision about how to respond to them.

I stay peaceful through each decision.

Traditions of Care

People in our family and our community have always taken care of the old and infirm. I'm doing what others before me have done. I expect my children to do the same. It's our tradition.

I'm proud of the way we look after each other. It's not easy, but we do it. Just like the mail carrier delivers mail. You can count on it. We don't want anyone to be needlessly miserable, so we take care of whoever needs help. We bring them things to eat. We run errands for them. We take them to the doctor. If need be, we bathe them and feed them. Everyone pitches in. If one person wears out, someone else takes a turn. In the end, if somebody needs professional services, we get that taken care of as well. No one has to go it alone.

We take care of each other the way we always have.

Healing Music

I wonder how I'd get through some days if it weren't for music. When my loved one's attitude or condition gets on my nerves, when no one seems to be cooperating, when tears start to come, I have my special songs to soothe me. They give me comfort, healing, energy, even joy sometimes.

Today might be a good day to listen to some of my favorite music, maybe even sing or play a few pieces myself. I could close my eyes and let myself swim in the sound of it. It would feel so good. I can start with music that matches my mood and then ease into other music that lifts me higher if I want. The music won't change my circumstances, but my soul will feel lighter, my spirit renewed.

Music melts my troubles and makes my day.

Gifts and Strengths

I know the last thing my loved one wants is for someone to feel sorry for her. I try not to do that, but at times I agonize over how much she has lost. My heart hurts when I look at her and see the way she suffers. I want her pain to go away.

There is a fine line between genuine compassion and pity. With compassion, I am lovingly attentive to her and I try to understand what she is going through. I let her know I care and offer assistance. I stick with her through the ups and downs and hold her in high regard. By contrast, pity sees her as diminished. Compassion is more respectful. It doesn't assume she is helpless even though she is experiencing great losses. It honors her strengths that have not gone away. In fact, some of her strengths may have grown through this experience. I marvel at the gifts she has to carry her through.

Compassion helps me tune in to both my loved one's suffering and strengths.

I'm Furious

I get so angry at the people who are supposed to be taking care of my loved one. I want them to come up with better answers. I want them to fix what's wrong. If they were doing their job, they'd be on top of this and she'd be better.

Of course, even when professionals do their best, that's no guarantee my loved one will improve. That's what I want, of course—my loved one to be healthy again. I'm so angry that her health problems are destroying her life and creating havoc in mine. I am outraged! Yet, I may not be able to change the state of her health, not even with the best of help. And that's hard to face. I want to keep hoping, trying. But I'm not sure what's realistic here. My fury clouds my thinking. Maybe my first task is to admit that what I'm really angry about is the loss and uncertainty I'm facing. I'm scared. It might help to say a prayer or talk over the situation with an understanding friend.

I pray for acceptance and wisdom.

Obligation

People do so much for me, I'll never be able to pay them back. I feel so guilty about accepting all this help. I've never wanted to depend on anyone.

Where did the rule come from that I have to pay everything back? A gift is a gift. Others want to help; so would I if I were in their shoes. Letting them help me doesn't mean there's something wrong with me. It means I recognize that others have something I need right now and I'm willing to let them express their goodness. I don't have to be superhuman. Knowing when to depend on others is also a strength. By receiving, I allow others to give. Honoring and appreciating their strengths and their generosity is the gift I give back to them.

I graciously and gratefully accept what others offer.

Laughing

It's a good thing I can laugh. So much is somber and stressful when someone is ill or disabled, I have to be able to laugh to get through the long days and weeks. In fact I could use more laughter.

A funny book or movie can loosen me up. Certain people I know automatically make me smile. Children especially tickle me. I can even get a good laugh from the goofy mistakes my loved one makes or that I make. Overall, I manage better when I hang around people and things that get my funny bone going. When I get too serious for too long, I almost forget how to laugh. In that case, I have to give myself a jump-start. One way is to "practice" laughing—literally to lie on my back and rapidly repeat "ha ha ha ha ha ha ha" several times. That gets my laugh muscles working every time.

I exercise my funny bone every day.

A Breaking Point

Life will be going along from day to day and I'm coping as best I can, and then one day something "small" happens—like the clothes bar in my closet suddenly snapping in two. Hangers and shirts and belts lie mangled in a clump on the floor. The mess reminds me of my whole situation: Since I've been caregiving, my life has snapped in two and I can't imagine enduring another minute of it.

This is a time to call the kindest person I know, the one I won't have to explain anything to. I'll just say that I'm struggling and this person will know what to do and will do it. And that act of kindness will sustain me until I can find a grain of strength in myself to go on. It will reassure me I'm not all alone. Supported by kindness from another, I will find it easier to recognize and admit that I've been "enduring" too long. I'll be able to see that I need to make some adjustments in the way I'm living.

When it feels like too much, it is.

Time for Prayer and Meditation

I'd like to pray more, meditate every day, be a more spiritual person...but who's got the time? My days are so full, I barely get done what I have to. I don't have time for long meditations or prayers. Yet I like the sense of peace they bring.

When I do take some time to get quiet and connect with my spiritual resources, the rest of my day goes better. I feel more peaceful. It works best if I set aside the same time every day. Then it becomes a habit. I may not get to it every single day, but I'm more likely to if it's in my routine. I use some inspirational reading materials to help me get into the right frame of mind. To help me follow through on my plans for this daily spiritual activity, I talk them over with a friend or spiritual guide and ask for support. I could even find someone to pray and meditate with me. However I do it, the rewards are great. Both my loved one and I feel the positive effects.

I take time for prayer and meditation every day.

Toughness

I don't want to accept the changes I see in my loved one. She's always been very capable and now she's losing some of her abilities. I can't believe this is happening. If we both stand tough, maybe we can hold it off.

We've gotten through a lot of things by standing tough, and I know our refusal to give in to this condition will help us now. But our determination to keep trouble at bay doesn't change the fact that she has health problems that are affecting her life and mine. I can't deny that. I wish she didn't have to go through this. It's hard to face. But it's better if I don't try to collude with her and pretend it's not happening. Part of being tough is facing reality and taking on what we need to take on. I'd better work with her to learn all we can about her condition and how to deal with it.

Toughness is not blindness.

When I'm Ill

On the days when I'm sick, it's hard to tell who needs more care. I can't do as much on those days and yet I don't want my loved one to feel neglected.

When I'm sick, I'm tempted to neglect my own needs and keep doing everything as usual. But it's important for me to take good care of my own health as well as my loved one's. If I don't, my condition may deteriorate, and I'll be even less able to provide care. I might also endanger my long-term health. If I continue to push myself when I'm not feeling well, I'm likely to get sicker and also give poorer care. I may get impatient, make mistakes, and end up doing more harm than good. When I'm sick, I remember to tend to my own health. I ask for help on those days. I expect less of myself. I seek appropriate consultation about my condition and take necessary remedies.

My health is a treasure and I intend to keep it.

Gathering In

The demands of caregiving keep me constantly in a giving mode. My loved one needs help. The family calls for information. The case worker wants to get together. I scatter my energy every which way, all day long. I feel disconnected from myself.

When I feel that scattered, I need a gathering-in time at day's end. I sit still and bring home my dispersed thoughts, my fractured energy. Like a mother hen huddling her flock, I call together all the busy activities of my mind under my wings and settle them down for the night. I rest them in the warmth and shelter of home. Now I'm back with myself, collected, calm. After a good night's rest, I can move back out to give again.

I respect the rhythms of giving out and gathering in.

Getting Around

I don't like to depend on outside help all the time, yet it's hard to get around when I have to transport my loved one. It takes so much time just getting to and from the car, let alone getting in and out of it, and I have to be so watchful. I get impatient and worn out. Sometimes it feels like it's not worth all the effort, so we don't go.

But getting out is important. We have appointments to get to and we simply need a change of scenery now and then. If I choose carefully, I can arrange to travel when I'm most rested. I can anticipate the extra time needed and not be rushed. I can think of the trip as an adventure, preparing myself to expect surprises or side trips. If I relax and create a positive attitude before we go, we'll both be calmer and more efficient in our movements.

I handle our traveling with ease and joy.

All That Is Human

Sometimes I feel such admiration for the person I'm caring for, I think my heart is going to burst. When I see the depth of her struggle, her continuing courage, and the learning that has gone on, I want to kneel in awe.

Watching my loved one go through so much has not only increased my love for her, it has raised my appreciation for what it means to be human. I've seen her experience the range of human possibility, from anguished despair and fury to genuine heroism. In a different way, my experience has been just as intense and wide-ranging. It's all there in each of us: the fullness of being human. Caregiving has plunged me into the center of this painful and glorious experience. I feel privileged.

> *I'm grateful to know intimately*
> *the richness of being human.*

Autonomy

I'm never quite sure how much to do for my loved one. When should I take over the decisions and decide what's "good" for her? Should I insist on things being done for her protection that she doesn't want done?

I know there are no easy answers to these questions. I don't want to interject my standards just so I can feel I've done the "right thing." Yet, I also don't want to see harm come to her because she can't protect herself. When she can't decide for herself, I make decisions that are as close as possible to what she would want. To do that, I have to look beyond my preferences to see through her eyes as best I can. Of course, if following her preferences will add more difficulty to my life, I must decide whether I'm willing to accept the added burden.

I carefully balance my loved one's autonomy
with my desire to do good.

Tender Tears

Tears can be healing, but they don't always come. Even when the sadness is deep, there are times when either my loved one or I can't cry. Something in our upbringing trained us to hold back tears. We couldn't release them even if we wanted to.

I know we can't borrow anyone else's tears, but sometimes I take a tear from my loved one's cheek and put it on my own or take one of mine and put it on his. That little act of sharing tears has a softening effect. Tears do that, they soften what's hard. Of course, it can feel like my insides are going to burst when I cry, but once the tears are shed, nothing is held back anymore. The pain is out in the open. The tightness and toughness are released. Tears water the heart so love can grow.

I welcome the tenderness of tears.

The Eyes of the Soul

When I see my loved one's body deteriorating, something in me recoils. What once seemed so beautiful has lost its attraction. I'm embarrassed that I'm taken aback by it and inclined to pull away from her.

I suppose my reaction is normal though. There is a natural beauty in each part of creation when in its prime. We admire and try to preserve this natural beauty. When it slips away, we reluctantly watch it change. We cling to the beauty we witnessed in full bloom. I am patient with myself when changes in my loved one hint of deterioration. I allow myself to get used to them over time, and I look for new kinds of beauty. Just as an artist can use sensitive photos and paintings to show the marvels of shriveled skin or limp hair, I can use the eyes of my soul to perceive a kind of beauty I would otherwise miss.

> *I explore the changes in my loved one*
> *with the eyes of my soul.*

Stuck Thinking

Sometimes a situation will come up that I just can't see my way out of. The course seems set, it's out of my control, and I don't like where it's going. I go over it in my mind again and again, and I can't see any other options...but I'm sure there must be some.

When I get that stuck, I've dug a deep ditch for my thinking. I need a derrick to pull myself out. At that point, my imagination is my best friend. Getting playful can help. I can close my eyes and see my problem as a huge balloon—and then let the air out of it. Or I can relax deeply and pretend I'm walking down a hallway. I come to a door labeled "answer" and explore what's behind it. When I get imaginative and playful like a child, I can think more intuitively and "can'ts" disappear.

> *Today I'll let my imagination lift me out of any mental ruts I'm in.*

Wishing for an End

I have terrible thoughts sometimes. I get so tired of taking care of my loved one and of all that it has meant for our lives that I just want it to end. It would be easier for both of us if he would die. But I feel so guilty for thinking like that.

It's not surprising, though, that such a thought would come to mind. It has been a challenging ordeal. Sometimes death seems like a more sane and peaceful solution. That's just the reality—it does seem that way. Not that I wish death on my loved on. What I'm wishing for is an end to all this misery. At times, I don't see any other way for that to happen. I feel a sense of despair, as though giving up is the only answer. When I honestly admit such feelings to myself, and maybe to a good friend or to my Spiritual Power, I don't feel guilty. Instead, I find my own dampened spirit in need of understanding and consolation. I tend to it gently.

My beleaguered spirit deserves a little kindness and comfort on such a long journey.

Being an Advocate

When others look at my loved one, they do not see what I see. They see his limitations and make assumptions about what he can or can't do based on appearances or diagnoses. I see his whole being and all his possibilities. I wish they'd take time to get to know him and understand all that he is capable of.

If I want people to discover his possibilities, I need to become his advocate. But in doing so, it's important to be patient with other people who don't know as much about his situation as I do. I need to teach them about his disease and what he can do. In some cases, I may need to insist that changes be made in the way he receives care. But I don't have to be responsible for all this teaching and advocating myself. I can participate in organizations that offer education about his condition or that help shape policies which could benefit him. In so doing, I will be helping not only my loved one but other people with similar problems.

I am glad I can be my loved one's advocate.

Kind Angels

I worry sometimes and think I'm so alone. But to my surprise, kind people have come through for me over and over again. They are angels—wonderful people who care, people who just come in and do what needs to be done. Or they say just the right word I need to hear or come up with an idea right when I need it. I wouldn't get through this experience without these special angels.

I don't know why I should be surprised. People want to be helpful, and each person has a multitude of experiences and skills to offer. It's good to know I don't have to rely just on my own resources. I can look around and watch for the angels.

I am thankful for all the angels who see me through.

Strength

It isn't often my loved one can be the strong one. Most of the time, I'm the one who has to carry the load. Since his reserves are low, I have to keep up my own strength so I can help him through the rough times.

But I'm glad I can be there for him. I have found inside myself an ocean of physical, emotional, and spiritual strength—more strength than I ever imagined I had. I want him to be able to depend on me. I want to do what I can to ease the pain. But on the days when my reserves are low, he'll sometimes come through with a show of strength. His very willingness to give a little support so touches me that I'm sustained for another day. But I know I can't depend on it regularly. To keep up my own strength, I make sure I have a deep well of other support that I can draw upon—friends, respite services, my Spiritual Power, whatever will restore me and keep me as strong as I need to be.

I am grateful for my strength.

Under Attack

People get mad at me. No matter how hard I try to do the right thing, either my loved one or the people involved in her care find fault with me. If I let them bother me, my blood pressure jumps sky high.

But when I stay calm and confident, their anger doesn't get to me. I treat it like an erupting geyser. I watch with interest, but keep at a safe distance so it doesn't harm me. Their anger is their anger, not mine. I don't have to let it in, nor defend myself against it. I have other choices. I can walk away. I can let them vent but not take their comments personally. I can tell them how their actions affect me. But I'm careful not to attack them in return or make them wrong. That may feel like "justice" in the short run, but why risk getting sucked into their way of doing things, which I so despise? I'm better off holding fast to my own internal strength and serenity and going on about my business.

I stay calm in the middle of other people's storms.

Dark Moods

When my loved one is down in the dumps, I try to keep my spirits up and be the determined cheerleader for him. I feel responsible for keeping a positive outlook no matter what happens. There are days when that's easy and I'm glad I can do it, but some days I don't have a single positive thought or feeling. My own spirits need lifting. If I act cheerful, I feel phony. Yet I'm afraid that if I'm not keeping my chin up at all times, we'll lose ground.

Maybe expecting myself to be "up" all the time is expecting too much. If being cheerful seems like hard work, I can just let go of the effort. I can be authentic by acknowledging that I'm feeling down temporarily and I can trust that the mood will pass. If either of us gets stuck in a prolonged dark mood, I know professional help is available.

I accept the ebb and flow of our moods.

Defiance

I've always relied on my loved one for certain things. Her humor, her creativity, her strength are all invaluable parts of our relationship. I don't want her to change. I don't want our relationship to change.

I feel a little like a defiant child. I want to cry out, "No, no, no." I want things to remain the same. In a way, this feeling of resistance to change is like my childhood defiance, because I'm not getting what I want. Something important to me is being taken away. But just as I am patient with an upset child who has to give up something precious, I am patient with myself in my time of loss and defiance. Anger and resistance and tears make sense. My life is changing in painful ways.

I comfort myself in these trying times.

Creative Projects

I have a number of creative interests, but since I've been spending my time caring for my loved one, I've let some of them drop. I miss being able to design or make things or do the kind of writing or music-making I enjoy.

My loved one has always had creative interests as well. I wonder if we could create something together. She may not be able to contribute a lot to the process, but on her better days, she might find it very satisfying to participate in a creative project. Besides, knowing that she will help me could be just the inspiration I need to work on it. We'll get to spend time doing something together that gives us a sense of accomplishment as well as a pleasant way to connect with each other.

Today I will do something creative with my loved one.

Delivering Bad News

News comes along that I know my loved one won't want to hear, like the need to move him to a nursing home or the news of a friend's death. I feel both sad and anxious about telling him. I don't want him to have to go through any more misery.

My tendency is to soft-pedal the news, in part because I fear his reaction. He may get angry. He may refuse to accept the news. He may despair. I'm afraid I'll get swallowed up in the immensity of his response. Yet he must be told, and so I tell him. I give the news gently but clearly. There must be no doubt in his mind about its reality. Then I allow him room to have his full range of feelings. If he attacks me as the messenger, I don't take it personally. I give him time to let the news settle in. If he refuses to accept the situation, I firmly move forward with any decisions the news requires, gently reassuring him as best I can.

I am strong when I need to be, out of love.

False Hope

The health care workers gave us lots of hope in the beginning. After treatment, they said, my loved one would be doing much better. It hasn't worked out like that. Yes, there was improvement, but not what we expected. I'm angry. I don't think they did what they could have for him, or else they lied.

I want so much for my loved one to be his old self. I expect the people in health care to have answers and to tell me exactly how things are going to turn out. I want them to give excellent care. Ultimately, I want them to do magic, to make this whole thing go away. I can't stand watching my loved one in this condition. Yet, I realize that there are no absolute answers. It's best if I make peace with that. I need to keep insisting that the best care be given, but I can't expect the health care workers to be magicians or to know exactly how much "hope" to give anyone. No one's condition or treatment comes with a guarantee.

I listen for hope but don't expect guarantees.

Extreme Reactions to Stress

The stresses of caregiving bring out the worst in people. If someone has a tendency toward impatience or carelessness or controlling behavior, it gets exaggerated. Everyone gets on each other's nerves.

Under the strains of caregiving, nobody's going to be a model of perfection. When a tense situation erupts, it's best if I remember that truth as quickly as I can, then forgive myself and move on. I can't afford to carry around lingering resentments. They only fuel my stress level. Of course, I can ask for what I want and set limits so that others' behavior doesn't make my life more difficult. Or I can suggest that we all lighten up a little. But it especially helps if I remember that everyone, myself included, may not be up to top performance in trying times. I am less likely to judge anyone harshly or demand more than what is reasonable.

> *I give myself and others a little slack
> when the stress mounts.*

Slipping Faith

I try to have faith that everything is going to turn out all right, that I'll be strong through it all, that the suffering of my loved one will be minimal. I try to believe in a God or some other kind of Spiritual Power, but I don't see things turning out in a way that seems right. Some days I don't know what to believe in.

I guess I want a higher being who will fix everything, who agrees with how I think things should be. That probably isn't very realistic. At least things aren't working out that way. The best I can do some days is to admit I don't have a clear sense of what to believe in and let that be enough. The not knowing can be unsettling and I'm tempted to say I have a strong faith because I'm supposed to. But I can't pretend when I'm this confused and uncertain. I can just be with my doubt and let that be my prayer.

My Spiritual Power is at home in the unknown.

Sudden Sadness

Sadness wells up at the strangest times. In a meeting, riding a bus, or shopping in the grocery store—suddenly I am hit by a surge of sorrow. It's not a time or place where I want my feelings to be on exhibit, and I don't know what to do with them.

But nobody objects if you have a runny nose, even in public, so I can hide my crying by letting the tears drain down my sinuses. Or I can step into a restroom and have a private cry. I don't have to hold back my feelings entirely. That's too much work and it kills something in me. I may not want anyone else at the moment to be aware of my sorrow, but I don't want to suffocate it either. My sadness tells me what I have loved and what I have lost. Sometimes I choose to share my tears with those around me. By showing them a little of my tender feelings, I keep my heart open, and I help others open theirs, too. My tears are part of my story as a caregiver, and my story is who I am.

I allow in the sadness and let the tears flow.

The Gift of Self

It's ironic when I think about it. I'm giving so much to my loved one, and I'm glad I can give, but it has taken a huge toll on me. I've given more than I could ever have imagined possible. The odd part is that, in the end, I will lose everything. He will likely die before I do, and for all my giving, I can't stop that from happening.

My giving has to be all from the heart now. I give out of love and respect. I give so that my loved one can be as comfortable and happy as possible. I do not do it for a return or reward. Some days there are neither of these, at least not that I can see. My own giving is the biggest gift I receive. Through that, I am discovering my capacity for caring profoundly, feeling deeply, and finding patience beyond what I thought possible. I am experiencing a wondrous new sense of presence with myself when I am fully there with my loved on. I can expect losses, but I will not be empty.

As I give, I receive more of who I am.

Appreciating the Gifts

Every time another piece of bad news comes along, my heart sinks. I get sad, discouraged, sometimes even depressed. I keep wondering why I have to have so much trouble in my life. It seems like there is one new problem after another.

I don't know that I have to label everything that happens as a "problem" or "bad news." What if, instead, I regarded them as opportunities to grow? In fact, almost every situation that comes along contains a gift if I'm open to seeing it. The troubles that my loved one and I are experiencing have brought out the kindness in so many people. Our problems have also prompted me to learn some new skills, use my creativity in new ways, and develop more compassion. I've discovered resources I didn't know about. I've found strength I didn't know I had. Even though I face some tough circumstances, I will handle them more easily if I remember to appreciate the good they bring.

I look for the gift in each situation that comes up.

Care for My Body

My body is feeling the effects of caregiving. I tend not to rest, exercise or eat as well as I should. I feel the strain. I'm tired and I have aches and pains.

It is just as important for me to care for my own body as it is to care for my loved one's. I am the person responsible for my own well-being and no one will take that on for me. I've heard about caregivers getting sick and even dying from the strains of caregiving. That's a good reminder to start taking better care of myself. If I stop what I'm doing right now, take a deep breath, and check in with myself for a moment, I can quickly identify one or two things I might do to take better care of my body. Maybe get a massage, back off on the sugar or caffeine, or go for a walk or climb stairs for aerobic exercise. Today is a good day to give my own body some care. I know I'll like the results.

I want the best for my body,
so I give it the best possible care.

Calming Movement

My mind gets easily scattered with all the responsibilities I have. My body gets tense. I want to be calm and grounded, but too often I'm harried and off-center.

Ancient traditions such as yoga, tai chi, and qi gong can help me settle down and be more peaceful. All of them start by inviting me to quiet myself, slow down, and bring my attention to the present. That alone starts me relaxing. Their gentle movements gather in my energy and direct my actions in a fluid way. I become centered, focused, integrated. Tension eases. I can reenter my day with more energy and with more of myself present to the tasks at hand.

I will find a book, tape, or class to guide me in basic centering exercises and do them often.

Caregiving as Escape

At times nothing matters to me except that my loved one needs me. I have other responsibilities, but I'll stay here with her anyway. I'll give her all I've got, no matter the price.

Yet I know that no one is absolutely needed. I am not indispensable. I am here because I choose to be. If my heart is in it, I'll give reasonably and lovingly. If I am here because I want to avoid facing the rest of my life, then I may be in a state of escape. If so, I will have more invested in my role as helper than it deserves. I will need my loved one to have problems so I can stay involved. To check my intentions, it may be wise to do an inventory of my motives. What is my heart's reason for being a helper? How am I handling my whole life while I give care? What do I get out of caregiving? What does it cost me? How willing am I to be "unnecessary?"

When I am honest with myself, I am able to give with a clearer intention.

Breaking the Monotony

Time passes so slowly some days. There isn't much to say and my loved one can't do very much. I just sit and watch the clock and get weary.

I want to liven up this numb feeling a little. I refuse to be a zombie. If none of my usual activities interests me, I can do one new thing to get me out of this stupor. Anything, just to break the monotony. Maybe even something a little silly, to get a smile going. How about making faces, like I did when I was a kid? I can call it "facial exercise" if I need an excuse to do it. Or maybe I can massage my ears or my hands or my arms for a few minutes. Or massage my loved one. How about singing or humming "This Old Man" or something else I learned as a kid? I'm sure I can think of something to do that's a little out of the ordinary.

I'll do something a little bit outrageous today—
just for fun.

Constantly Changing Plans

It's almost impossible to make personal plans. I never know from one day to the next what might happen with my loved one. A sudden increase in symptoms, a rescheduled treatment, a change in service providers—all these "surprises" keep the plans I try to make up in the air.

I don't like uncertainty. When I make plans, I like to stick with them. Especially when they include other people. I don't like having to call and cancel. I want to keep doing activities that are important to me, so I need to look for ways to reduce my anxiety about changing plans. I don't have to turn an inconvenience into a catastrophe. If I remember that each change is just one change and avoid thinking of it as part of a collection of changes, it may seem more manageable. I know I can handle one change of plans, so I go ahead and handle the one in front of me and trust that I can handle the next one just as well.

I am capable of adjusting to changes, one at a time.

Dream Wisdom

I'm sure there must be a solution to my present dilemma, I just don't know what it is. Even though I've tried many things, I can't seem to find the key.

Somewhere inside myself I know I can unravel this situation and find a way out. I could ask for help in my dreams before I go to sleep. Answers sometimes come to me that way. I also find answers sometimes in "daytime discovery dreaming." In a quiet, relaxed state, I close my eyes and imagine that I have a key in my hand—the key to my dilemma. I see myself walking down a long path in the woods until I find a building. I go inside and find a number of rooms. Their doors are closed. I try each door until I find the one my key fits. I walk in and look around. I see objects or people there to help me and I do whatever I'm prompted to do. When I am done, I might have a sense of the solution I am seeking, and I return to my fully awake state. I use my discovery to help solve my dilemma.

I welcome the wisdom of my subconscious mind.

Embarrassing Behaviors

Occasionally I am embarrassed by things my loved one does. I know her health problems affect her ability to act normally, so she can't help what she does. But I still find myself getting upset when she does certain things in the presence of friends.

It's odd, really, that her actions embarrass me. They are not my actions. They are hers. But I don't want people thinking badly of her or feeling sorry for her. I also tend to think that what she does reflects on me—guilt by association. Sometimes I keep people away from her, just to avoid all this. But that's unfair to her and to me. We need the company and support of others. I can use discretion, of course, but for the most part, it is all right if other people get to experience her difficult behaviors just as I do. She is who she is, and I am not responsible for her behavior, nor do I need to cover up for it. She has gifts to give to others even in her off times.

I invite others to know my loved one as I do.

Revved Up

I can't relax. Even when I have time, I can't do it—I just keep going. There's always something to do. I'd like to stop, to spend time watching the moon or playing with the dog or taking a nap. But it's almost as if I've forgotten how. I'm so revved up, I can't shift into idle.

The downshifting is rough, but if I give myself enough time, I relax eventually. However, if I try to get to idle too quickly, the change is even harder to take. My whole system is still geared up and wants to push on. Still, if I want to relax, I have to be willing to go through this time of adjustment, to experience the jarring change and give my system time to catch up. It's very uncomfortable at first, but once that rocky period passes, I sink at last into the ease of being on pause. For a while, I'm not driven; I just forget my cares and notice how good it feels just to be alive.

The downshifting may be rough at first,
but the rest at the end is worth it.

Safety Concerns

I worry about my loved one's safety. What if he falls? What if his other caregivers fail to take proper precautions? What if he has a problem and no one is around to help him? I'm afraid for him.

Yet I can't be with him every minute. And even if I could, I couldn't protect him completely. I remember my parents and teachers worrying about me the same way when I was little. They tried to protect me from all dangers, and ultimately they couldn't. I guess the desire to protect those we love is a natural instinct. I'm glad I'm able to look out for my loved one. But it's one thing to take reasonable precautions, it's another to obsess about potential dangers all day long. If I do all I can to provide a safe environment for him, I let my mind rest, knowing that I can't control everything in his life. If a problem arises, I'll deal with it then.

I keep my mind safe from worry.

Satisfaction

I do many things for my loved one, and she appreciates my help. As a result, she is able to do things she couldn't do otherwise. She is able to maintain some degree of independence and continue doing things that are important to her. It would be nice to get showered with thanks for what I do, but that's not why I do it.

When my loved one is doing relatively well, people aren't always aware that I've had any hand in that. I like this behind-the-scenes role. I feel proud that I've made it possible for her to find more enjoyment in her life and to do things that bring her attention, recognition, or appreciation. Sometimes I step back, watch, and smile. I know I've done well when she is doing so well that she forgets that she must sometimes rely on me. My best thank-you comes from her happy face.

I'm glad I can help my loved one feel self-satisfied.

Soul Sense

Sometimes while I'm tending to the care of my loved one, I'm aware of the presence of something beyond his body—his soul or spirit. I get just a glimpse, but it's a sacred moment for me. My own spirit is awakened. I know we are together in ways that are outside the physical realm. I want to hold on to those moments.

During much of my mundane daily schedule, I lose track of that sense, that connection, yet it never leaves me completely. Once I have known another's soul, I'm never a stranger to it again. On dark days, I find solace in these experiences. I long to revisit them. I know I cannot make them happen, but if I choose, I can still myself, settle into the knowing of my own soul, and let what comes come. Even turning my attention to the promise of a soul experience comforts me.

I take comfort in soul meeting soul.

Survival Kit

I wish someone would give me a caregiver survival kit. I was thrown into this without much preparation. Some days I feel like I'm drowning. I need a few essentials to hang on to.

If I could design a "survival kit" for myself, what would it contain? How about a healthy eating routine and enough rest to ensure survival for the long haul? Time to connect with my Spiritual Power? Contact with one or more supportive friends? A journal to record my thoughts? Exercise? Time with nature? Inspirational reading? "Escape" reading? A favorite sitcom? I would include whatever I decide is basic to my survival and keep it handy. It might help to tell a friend or my support group about my "kit" and ask them to remind me if I forget to use it. I could also post the list of contents on my refrigerator to refresh my memory every morning. My survival depends on remembering.

I have a survival kit to keep me sane and healthy.

Talking about Death

I don't like to think about death, but when my loved one's condition takes a turn for the worse, it comes to mind. Death seems to be just outside the gate then, waiting for its entrance cue. I try to keep it out of my mind, but I know death will come eventually. I try to prepare myself, but there is no way to rehearse for death.

Death is an awful thing, yet it is evident everywhere in creation. When I allow myself a glimpse of it, I am both repelled and curious. Because I am repelled, I try to protect my loved one, and myself, from it. But perhaps I should engage my curiosity and enter into the mystery of death when I sense its nearness. If my loved one were willing, I could tell her my reactions, from fear to fascination, and invite her to tell me about hers. There can be no rehearsal for death, but I can bear witness and live with her through her journey toward dying.

The imminence of death invites intimate conversations about dying.

When Things Go Wrong

When something goes wrong, I'm tempted to blame myself. If a helper doesn't show up, if a treatment doesn't work, if my loved one's condition gets worse, I start to think I've failed in some way.

Of course, I'm not responsible for everything that goes on in my loved one's life. I am making many choices and doing many tasks related to his care, but I can't control how everything is going to turn out. Even when I do have a fair amount of control, I'm not likely to get perfect results. When something doesn't work out as expected, I don't want to spend a lot of time rehashing what went wrong. If I see a way to make some course corrections to prevent further problems, it's wise to make them; but beyond that, I let it go and put my attention on the next thing in front of me. I'm not to blame for everything.

I waste energy if I crucify myself over things that go wrong.

Trouble in our Relationship

I love the person I'm caring for, but our relationship is not perfect. We've had a few tough exchanges that have left big scars. He needs a lot of support from me now, but I'm not always comfortable giving it. I would like to see these troubling aspects of our relationship resolved first.

I keep hoping that, since he needs me and I've helped him so much, he'll treat me the way I want to be treated. I think to myself, Maybe now, if he sees how kind I am to him, he'll want to make up for the past. But he is who he is. If I expect him to change, I am setting myself up for disappointment. Even if he wanted to, his health problems might not let him. Since I have no control over whether he changes or not, it is more helpful if I focus on accepting him as he is. That I can do something about, and it helps me feel more peaceful about taking care of him.

I accept what I cannot change,
and I courageously change what I can.

Deep Breathing

When the days get long and I have to sit for many hours—waiting for news, waiting for changes, waiting for decisions—I get weary. My mind slides into a stupor. Tension settles into every bend in my body. I barely breathe.

Maybe what I'm missing is my breath. I'm not getting enough of it. My whole body has collapsed around my lungs and the tension is holding them in check. A deep wide breath is a good way to start loosening things up. I fill up my lungs like a huge balloon all the way from my belly to my neck. My chest and tummy expand to make room. Then I hold that breath for as long as I can and let it out in one big blast. Three or four big breaths like that help to stretch out my tight muscles and get lots of oxygen moving through my body. If I do ten of them, I feel even more awake and relaxed.

I breathe deeply and live.

Demanding Too Much of Myself

I demand more of myself than anyone else. It's as if I think I should be suffering since my loved one is. Sometimes I drive myself far beyond what's reasonable.

Of course, adding more suffering to my life isn't going to make things better for him. It only makes me more miserable. I run the risk of thinking myself "noble" or "righteous" somehow, as if I'm a better person because I take on more and more suffering. In the end, this false nobility has a high cost. I become overtired, irritable, resentful. Eventually, my spirit falters. So does my health. I am unable to give good care when I give so much of myself over to suffering. I would be better off to lighten the pressure I place on myself and give up noble suffering in exchange for sanity.

My job is not to suffer but to care for my loved one and for myself.

New Remedies

Just when I think I understand the various treatments available for my loved one, I hear about something new. I read about a new medication, a revived herbal remedy, or a mental or spiritual exercise that promises a breakthrough. I get my hopes up. Then I get confused. I don't know what to believe or which path to follow, and neither does my loved one.

Of course, there are no absolutely right answers anywhere and every choice involves some risks. I make the most conscientious choices I can about my loved one's care. I try to stay up to date on health remedies, though I can't pursue every new approach that comes along. I weigh the information I gather. I consult with people I trust. I take into account the needs and preferences of my loved one and myself. I pray. Then I choose. I can do no better than that and I don't second-guess myself.

I trust myself to select wisely among treatment options and stay open to learning more.

Changes in Appearance

My loved one doesn't look the same anymore. Changes in weight, skin condition, muscle tone— lots of things have changed. Sometimes I glance at this person I've known so well, and it's almost as if I see a stranger. I'm reluctant to admit it, but I sometimes recoil from what I see.

I don't like being affected by such things as physical appearance, but there it is, right in front of me. I can't help but react. The disturbing feelings can be huge. I'm glad I can remember that I'm not bad for having these feelings. They're a normal reaction to such a big change. They will pass in time. For now, I just accept being "normal." Writing my feelings in my journal or telling them to my support group helps me sort them all out. And I ask my Spiritual Power to help me see beyond appearances to the unchanging soul of my loved one.

I accept that I have strong feelings
about the changes I notice.

Choking Back Grief

I've lost so much since my loved one has developed health problems. What we can do together is limited. My time is not my own. We've had to get rid of some belongings to accommodate the changes he has gone through. It seems like the losses never stop. I want to cry, but once I start, I'm afraid the tears won't stop. I have to stay strong.

The pain of grief seems unbearable. I want to avoid it. It takes over my whole body and I can't contain it. I'm afraid of it—afraid I'll lose control. I want to stay strong. But inside I feel a deep sadness. Each of the things I've lost has meaning to me, and I miss them all. It's only right to mourn their passing from my life. Deep grief may weaken my stronghold for a time, but it will not consume me in the end. My tears will be a cleansing—painful, yes, but freeing. I won't have to hold on so tight to choke back my grief anymore. I can comfort myself even as I cry, and feel the relief of grief expressed.

I let grief take its course and gently comfort myself.

Bitterness

The members of our family have changed since we started taking care of our loved one. Some refuse to deal with it, some are jealous of the attention our loved one gets, and some are downright mean. I have become bitter about the situation.

I wish we could come together as a family and rally around our loved one, but chances are it won't happen—at least not with everyone. Some family members don't have the ability to cope with this situation, and they will never do the things I wish they'd do. However, I don't want to spend my time thinking about that. It hurts and upsets me too much. Instead, I accept the fact that they are how they are. I may not like it, but I can't change them. Rather than letting it drag me down, I put my bitterness in the hands of my Spiritual Power and focus my attention on what I can contribute to the situation and on the benefits that are mine because of it.

Bitterness is a burden I refuse to carry.

Beyond Reasoning

From time to time, I get an inclination to do something for my loved one that seems "unreasonable," yet just feels right. My mind says it can't be done, but my heart wants to go ahead with it.

I trust my intuition. If I get an internal nudge to ask for a service even though it's probably not available, I do so because I assume something good will come from my request. And who knows? I might even get what I ask for! If I am prompted to take my loved one someplace even though I doubt she can get in, I trust that somehow she'll get in or else we'll discover something good for her while we're there. For example, even though she can't climb the stairs, we might discover that the people she is going to see have moved to a street-level unit. I'm continually delighted by the pleasant surprises that come along when I'm willing to follow the inner directions I get.

What seems "unreasonable" ain't necessarily so.

Crabbiness

I want to carry out my caregiving role with grace and love, but I don't always do so. In fact, some days I'm shocked at how crabby and nasty I become. I say things I never imagined myself saying, taking my frustration out on others. It's unsettling to see such an ugly side of myself.

I think to myself, That can't be me saying that. But yes, it's me! I'd rather not admit it. It doesn't match what I think I should be saying or what other people expect. It takes me by surprise to hear myself being so cross and unkind. I thought the hardest challenge in caregiving was going to be accepting my loved one in his worst moments, but accepting myself at my worst is even more difficult. He has an excuse—a health problem. I have none, except maybe exhaustion. But excuses are irrelevant. The reality is that I have my moments of nastiness. The question is: Can I love myself anyway?

I do my best to avoid unkind behavior,
but I'm still lovable when I don't succeed.

Addictions

When I feel stressed out over the responsibilities of caregiving, I'm tempted to turn to one of my favorite pacifiers: food, TV, sex, busyness, talking, caffeine, nicotine, alcohol. Any of these can consume my day if I let them. They are addictive. I lose myself in them and they cost me dearly. And yet the stress keeps coming back. I wish I could stop.

I know I'm not the only one. Lots of people get hooked on something. But I've read that when people learn to deal with their addictions, they become more peaceful. Maybe I could find a way to deal with mine. I'd like some peace of mind. I could ask my doctor or a counselor for help or do some reading about addictions. With the help of my Spiritual Power, I can find strength to make changes. It's time I get myself back. I need all of me if I'm going to keep on going as a caregiver.

> *I do what is necessary to free myself*
> *from addictive behaviors.*

Being Authentic

I usually assume that my loved one and I have the same understanding about his condition and his needs, but sometimes I discover he's not taking proper care of himself. It's as if he refuses to admit that he's got a problem. If I bring it up, he dismisses my concerns. I feel hurt that he's not telling me what's going on.

My inclination is to pull back, bury the hurt, and hide my annoyance, although sometimes I do get angry with him. If he's having trouble accepting something or is feeling defiant, I wish he'd tell me so we can have an understanding. I don't like being left in the dark. I'm afraid. I dislike the distance between us. But I can't make him talk to me. And yet it doesn't help to ignore what's going on or to insist that he be realistic. What I can do is tell him how hurt and frightened and cut off I feel—not to push him to act, but simply to be honest.

The best care I can give myself is to be authentic.

Keeping Separate

I get so absorbed in my loved one's condition at times that I can hardly think of anything else. I feel his feelings, think his thoughts. When his stomach hurts, mine starts to hurt too. I have trouble separating myself from him.

Even though I want to care about him, I also want to have a life of my own. When I'm too closely tied to my loved one, my own sense of self disappears. It's like an umbilical cord binding us to each other. I can't let go. Maybe I could ask my imagination for help. I know that when I imagine doing something in a symbolic way first, it becomes easier to do the real thing. So in a quiet moment, I imagine this cord as it extends from the center of my belly to the center of his, keeping us firmly connected. I picture myself cutting the cord on both ends so I'm free again. Then I magically transform the cord into a rose: a reminder that my love for him, though a thing of beauty, does not mean living his life.

I love my dear one, but I am not him.

Commitment to Life

I get furious about the possibility of my loved one dying. It isn't fair that I might lose her. It isn't fair that her vitality and all that matters to her will be taken away. Something in me refuses to accept that. Somehow it shouldn't have to happen!

It makes sense to rage against death. Everything in my human nature strives to sustain life. I wish I could be more willing to appreciate death, and there are days when I can. But my fury about death is also part of my reality, and I cannot hide from it. I'm glad I have it. It's a sign I value life. It's a sign of my deep caring for my loved one and my desire that he have all the gifts life has to offer for a good long time yet. I know my angry defiance may not stop his death, but when it surges through me, I celebrate it as evidence of my commitment to life and love.

*My defiance about death awakens me
to my love of life.*

Long-term Realities

I'm surprised I've been caregiving this long. I keep expecting things to get better before long, so I have continued with most of my normal activities, even with my added caregiving responsibilities. I think to myself, Oh, I can handle it. But over time, I've gotten more and more tired and harried.

The days keep adding up, yet I haven't wanted to acknowledge that this situation may continue indefinitely. I keep thinking that if I can just bear up a little while longer.... But the truth is, this situation is likely to continue for a long time. It's time I design my life to meet that reality. I swallow hard when I think about the long haul. It's not what I expected. It's not what I prefer. Yet if I am to continue caregiving and keep from going under myself, I'd best take an inventory of the situation and see what I can get help with or set aside for the duration. My health and my sanity depend on it.

I adjust my activities and my expectations of myself to meet the realities of long-term caregiving.

Firmly Planted

I get so scattered in my thinking sometimes, it's as though my mind has taken flight. A wind could blow me away like a feather. I can't make a decision, I forget things, I can't connect with people. My feet feel like they are barely touching ground.

Sometimes it helps to literally put my feet on the bare earth, or at least solidly on the floor, and pay some attention to them. I allow myself to feel the ground or floor beneath my feet. I wiggle my toes—maybe even stomp my feet—so I can feel solidly connected to what holds me up. I close my eyes and imagine putting roots down from the bottom of my feet. This helps me get "grounded" again. I anchor the whole lower half of my body, and then the upper half, securing my stand against the winds of change.

With my feet firmly planted on the ground, nothing can blow me over.

Giving Physical Care

I have to do things for my loved one I never imagined myself doing. I help him with some of his physical needs that he can't manage for himself. It can be embarrassing, difficult, and unpleasant.

Of course, there was a time when my parents did similar things for me. Imagine how many diapers they changed and how hard they must have worked to toilet-train me. I couldn't do those things for myself, so they helped me over and over until I could manage on my own. They took care of me day by day in many other ways during my childhood—bathing me, dressing me, looking after me when I was sick. Now I take care of my loved one in some of the same ways. It's a good thing I had someone to take care of me when I needed help, and it's a good thing I can take care of my loved one. I'm glad we're all built with the natural tendency to look after one another.

I give care because it is in my nature to do so.

Impatience

I find myself getting very impatient and irritable at times. Things that normally wouldn't bother me really get to me now. Then I try even harder to be patient, which makes me even more tense. I end up crying or exploding.

I might be able to avoid this build-up of tension if I notice when I start to feel on edge. There is a good chance that simmering underneath that edginess is a bit of fear or anger or grief that I need to tend to. But just as likely, some physical problem may be causing my crabby mood. In the busyness of my life, I may be overlooking my body's signs that something is out of whack. Everything from PMS to prostate trouble to lack of sleep can make a person extra irritable or tense. I'm very attentive to my loved one's physical condition, but it's also important to tune in to my own. When I'm aware of my body's messages, I can take better care of myself. Then I feel better and have more patience.

I listen to my body and take care of myself.

Love of Family

Many things in our family have shifted since our loved one developed his problems. We've had to decide how to share responsibilities. As more is asked of everyone, we can get a little testy with each other.

At the same time, I appreciate my family more than ever before. Some of them have been especially wonderful. We've become closer as we've gone through all this together. And something about my loved one's health problems makes me appreciate even more the preciousness of each person's life. Even though we have times when we don't agree or when I don't like what someone is doing, I love my family. I do everything I can to keep in my heart that sense of preciousness I feel in my most tender moments. Even when I'm at odds with my family, I treat them with respect and care. I look for the best in all of them and forgive their weaknesses. I hope they do the same for me.

My heart is full of love for my family.

Guilt

When I notice how hard things are for my loved one, I feel guilty. I think I should be doing something more. I should be there more often, be more patient, try harder to get the services that are needed, contribute more financially.

Guilt can swamp me if I let it. It's easy to forget that I am making the best choices I can in my current circumstances. They are good enough. I am good enough. If I see ways to make changes for the better, I'll do that. But starting today, I'm going to drop the burden of guilt over any "shoulds" or "coulds." I'm going to let myself off the hook. Feelings of guilt may still surface, but when that happens I can gently remind myself that I'm doing things differently now and that my best is good enough.

I send guilt on its way and say goodbye.

Moves

Every time there is a need to move my loved one, I am flooded with concerns. Is this move a good idea? Will she be well cared for? Will the financial arrangements be clear and manageable? Will she be satisfied? I'd prefer we didn't have to go through this. I wish she could just be settled in one place for good.

But it might not be that way. We may have to adjust yet again. If so, staying calm can help the process be more peaceful. It helps to remember that nothing going on around me need disturb the peace within me. I bless the place she is leaving and bless the place she is going to. I've checked out the options as best I can, and I trust the decisions that have been made about the move. In her new place, I do what I can to help her be comfortable and make the best of the situation. I let go of the need to control whatever is out of my hands.

> *I bless each place my loved one lives*
> *and trust all will be well there.*

Ordinary Problems

I long for ordinary problems. A canker sore. A slow microwave. A spot on my pants. These I can handle. They seem almost pleasant after what I've been through. They would mean ordinary life has returned.

"Ordinary" isn't what it used to be for me. I have a different perspective now on what used to exasperate me. The smallest inconveniences once seemed intolerable. Now they seem as small as they actually are. After I've faced such big problems as surgeries and emergency room visits and questions of life and loss, I'd almost welcome the routine disturbances of a normal life. Who ever would have thought of a canker sore as a welcome change of pace?

In perspective, all problems are small.

On a Fast Train

Everything is moving too fast and I feel like I've lost control. Caregiving involves so many decisions to make and so many things to do, and there's not enough time or energy to get on top of it all. My life is a runaway train.

I guess it's time to have a talk with the Engineer. I don't think distance or speed matter much in this case. I can stop anywhere, anytime, close my eyes, and make contact with the One who "engineers" everything. When I do that, I automatically slow down and discover that I am the one going at full speed. I am the one who needs to slow down long enough to get a better sense of pacing. I am the one who needs to adjust my schedule and attitude to help me stay calm and efficient. Drawing on spiritual guidance, I can ride the rails peacefully and get done what is important.

I get things done and keep my sanity by staying in touch with the One who is timeless.

Positive People

Sometimes when I'm in a negative mood and start to complain, people complain with me. I'm sure they think they're helping me by agreeing with my complaints, but instead they just magnify my concerns and my bad mood. And then they add on a few of their own complaints. I end up feeling even more dissatisfied with the world.

I want to talk with positive people when I'm down in the dumps. Not that I want people to ignore my problems, but positive people have a way of putting a softer spin on them. They listen to me and empathize, but then they point out a brighter side to the problem, or they ask me thoughtful questions to help me come up with some solutions for myself. They help me move from making a complaint to making a request or making a change. I keep handy a list of positive people I can call on when I get bogged down.

I keep in close contact with positive people.

Simple Pleasures

I am exhausted. I give and give and give, and I feel like I have nothing left. I wonder how much longer I can keep going like this. And, at least for now, there is no one to give me much relief.

I need to do something today to replenish my energy, even if it's just something small. Maybe stopping to experience some simple pleasures would help. I could listen to a songbird and let it stir a song inside me. I could look at photos of children I love. I could touch a velvet pillow and enjoy its luxurious feel. I could wiggle my toes and watch them dance.

Simple pleasures delight and energize me.

Toughness and Softness

Caring for my loved one has both toughened me and softened me. I'm not always sure which side of me is called for in any given situation, but sooner or later it becomes clear. Sometimes I need both.

In some instances I've had to stand up to people or endure past what I thought were my limits. If I hadn't grown a few callouses, I would never have made it. I had to be strong so I could say yes or no emphatically. In other instances, my toughness had to stay parked in idle. I've had to soften up, become flexible, open my arms, and widen my lap. Over time, I'm learning to stay alert in each situation to see which is better to rely on, toughness or softness. I work to keep them in balance and with all the practice I am getting as a caregiver, I'm sure they'll both grow stronger.

My toughness and my softness provide needed balance as I care for my loved one.

Visits

When my loved one's condition is at its worst, I find it hard to visit her. I get so disheartened and sad. She isn't really herself and I feel helpless.

When I feel like that, I don't go alone. I ask family members or friends to go with me. Their company helps buffer the pain. It also gives me someone to talk with if my loved one can't communicate. It helps me to have others see how life is for my loved one. That way I know they understand what she's dealing with and what I'm dealing with as well. And if I break down emotionally, they can comfort me. Having someone with me gives me the courage to visit more often and cope with the challenges I face when I do.

I invite others to walk with me through the pain.

Confusion

I wish someone would help me figure out all the things I need to know to help my loved one. There is so much to learn about his condition and so much to understand about the systems involved in his care. I get a headache trying to make sense of it all.

When I get this confused, I can't think straight, so it helps me to take a break from thinking. I set thinking aside for a while and do something totally opposite. I may take a break and spend some time sitting with my loved one and enjoying a relaxing activity. If it's an activity he can do with me, all the better. I play with our pet, whip up a special beverage or snack to share, or sing a song—some pleasant activity that refreshes my spirit and reminds me of the heart reasons behind all the learning I have to do. After my break, I have a clearer mind and more energy to unravel the puzzles before me.

> *When my mind needs a break,*
> *I rest or do something I enjoy.*

Pity

When I see how much my loved one has lost, how even some basic functions are not under his full control, I feel a rush of pity. He was such a capable, active person, and now he has to be cared for in ways that must feel humiliating. I know pity is not what he needs, but sometimes it just sweeps over me.

If I look at what's behind this pity, I see that it comes from my respect for him. I value so much the person I know him to be. He has contributed a lot to my life and I am saddened to see his full capacity diminished this way. I mourn the slipping away of dignity, yet I cannot show pity. It will not serve him. Instead, I let it remind me of how much I value him and I focus on doing what I can to support his dignity. I gently transform my pity into appreciation. I keep vigil at the altar of his life, watching and fueling the flame of his spirit that still burns.

I hold my loved one in high regard.

Prayer

When I pray for my loved one, I sense the closeness of my Spiritual Power. I know my loved one prays, too. When we share some of our prayer experiences together, there is spiritual resonance between us.

Prayer is an activity of the soul that my loved one and I each do in a unique way. It tends to be such a private experience. Yet, done together, it unites our souls in their common hunger for union with the sacred. Whether we pray in silence or aloud, we both sense a presence greater than both of us. Fears diminish. We are showered with wisdom, love, hope—all those things that raise us above our limitations. We share a state of peace. Although we don't always have such profound experiences when we pray together, it is often very comforting.

Praying together draws us closer to each other and to our Spiritual Power.

Possessions

When people lose some of their ability to function, they often have to give up treasured objects. These items are no longer needed, or space for them is no longer available. Some may even pose a safety risk. As I watch my loved one release her possessions one by one, I realize more than ever that her significance is not in her external possessions.

Certain belongings have mattered a great deal to her. I tend to associate them with her, and it seems odd when they are no longer around. I know it's been hard for my loved one to give them up. She is sad about the loss, yet as things are stripped away, her essence becomes even more apparent and important. There is more of her and less of her things. This all takes some getting used to for both of us. I understand now that my possessions will not always be with me.

Neither my loved one's possessions, nor my own, define us.

Objective Perspectives

I can obsess about problems and lose all perspective. I can spend the whole day rehashing a conversation or second-guessing a decision I made or building a case against someone I consider at fault. I lose my ability to concentrate on what I'm doing because I'm so upset.

At times like these, I want the input of objective outsiders to help me achieve a saner perspective. My telephone becomes my lifeline. I have friends who will sympathize with me. I also have a few practical and sensible friends who help me see what I'm too close to to see. They don't tell me what to do, but ask, "Have you considered this...or that?" They help me find additional information and other resources. They support me in an honest and realistic way; they don't say things just to make me feel better. I still make my own choices, but I value and draw upon the thoughtful observations of my support system.

I cultivate and make use of my support system.

Repayment

My loved one wants to be independent. He doesn't like having to accept help from me, and he acts as if he is obliged to pay me back. I wish he could just accept what I offer.

I know he has to wrestle with this himself. I'm not in his shoes and I can't fully understand his need to "pay his own way." It is important to him to have as much control as he can over his life and not feel obligated. I can't take that feeling away. I can only offer my help in ways that respect his desire for independence. If he offers to pay me back in some way, I can graciously accept his offer or at least express genuine appreciation for his willingness. I can also notice and acknowledge other ways in which he gives to me. Just as I want him to accept what I offer, it's important that I accept his offerings. Then we can operate from mutual appreciation and respect.

> *I give what I'm able to give,*
> *but I'm also willing to receive.*

Rest

When my loved one naps, I think I'll be able to get a lot of work done. Since I don't have to be concerned about her needs, I try to pack in as much activity as I can. But by the time she wakes up, I feel exhausted and have little energy to attend to her.

I know that working to exhaustion while she naps is not healthy for me. I'm wearing out and losing the energy to do what I have to do. Maybe I could change this routine: I don't have to keep doing what I've always done. I know that when I'm rested, I feel better and do a better job. It only makes sense, then, to get some rest. What if I napped when she napped? Could that become my new routine? At first, I may feel a tug to work, afraid that I won't get everything done. But chances are, once I've rested I'll be more efficient. At the very least, I'll be more alert, energetic, and able to enjoy what I'm doing.

I honor my need to rest and refresh myself.

Redecoration

I've gotten to know every detail of my loved one's room. I know where the imperfections are in the walls and woodwork. I know where dust accumulates. The space gets oppressive after a while. The chairs are uncomfortable. The colors in the room have begun to wear on me.

A little redecoration might be in order. I may not be able to redo everything, but perhaps I could rearrange the furniture. Or maybe I could add a decorative shade pull or a colorful hanging or a photo display. Any small adjustment could help change the scenery. I want to maintain a warm living environment that doesn't feel stale or stifling. Adding decorative touches that give pleasure and comfort can go a long way toward making his room more livable. I'll feel less like I'm "stuck" there. Maybe he will, too.

I can dress up the room to give our senses a treat.

Reading Familiar Stories

Some of the great stories that have been written are fun to reread again and again, especially the children's classics. There is something about an old familiar story that feels like coming home. I enjoy reading stories like that, but I don't want to take time away from my loved one to do it.

I wonder if she might enjoy these stories like I do. I get a real warm feeling when I think of *Winnie the Pooh* or *Charlotte's Web* or *The Wind in the Willows.* They speak to the innocence and tenderness in all of us. They give gentle reminders of how people find their way through troubled times. I could get one of these books from the library and read it aloud. Or if these books are on tape, we could both listen. No doubt there are any number of books that would be enjoyable to share. I can ask friends or a librarian for ideas or ask my loved one, for that matter.

I will get a familiar book we can both enjoy and share it with my loved one.

Mutual Support

People don't understand how difficult it is to deal with my loved one's condition on a day-to-day basis. Sometimes when I talk about what happens, they act as if I'm making it up, as if it can't really be that bad. Or they dismiss it by saying they have bad days, too. I want someone to really listen to me, to let me know they genuinely understand what I'm dealing with.

If I want to be understood, my best bet is to find other people in similar circumstances. A clergy member or social worker might put me in touch with other struggling caregivers. Or I could join a caregiver support group offered through a social service agency, religious organization, or health care service. I could also go to information meetings offered through health care facility or organizations that serve people in my loved one's condition. When I find someone who's "been there," I don't feel so misunderstood or alone.

I seek others who understand for mutual support.

My Courage

I'm tempted to deny what's happening to my loved one. It just can't be so. There must be some mistake or some way out of this. I can't bear to believe his condition is as bad as they say.

Yet I want to be realistic and give him the support he needs. I start by calling on my Spiritual Power— my best source for wisdom and strength. Then I gather information about his condition, what he'll need, and what resources are available. I make sure I have a support system of family, friends, and others to stand by me. I set aside fear and draw from the well of courage that I have filled over a lifetime. And I trust that I will have everything I need to handle the challenges this situation brings.

When things look grim, I calm myself, pray, and remember my courage.

Rituals

When my loved one needs surgery or a new treatment or a new place to live, I become terrified. I have seen so many things go wrong that I imagine the worst. Fear takes hold of me and I can't sleep or think clearly. The sense of danger is immense.

In times like these, the comfort of a sacred ritual can soothe me and give me strength. It can be a simple, familiar one—lighting a candle, taking communion, donning a prayer shawl, burning sage, singing a favorite hymn. Or it might involve joining with others in communal rituals such as a worship service, a sweat lodge, or a hands-on healing ritual. There may be a leader or guide present to remind me of higher possibilities and help free me from my fears. Whether alone or with others, I find a peaceful sense of connection and protection from doing common rituals. For a long time afterward, they continue to nourish a feeling of trust that my loved one and I will be taken care of.

Rituals remind me where to place my trust.

Scars

My loved one has scars on his body. They show where he has been injured or where surgery was done. They are ugly in a way. They mar the beauty he was born with. But they mark moments of significance, too. Each one has a story.

My body has scars, too, and stories to go with them. Some of them tell of courage, some of foolishness, some of hope. They are records of my life journey. What if I told their stories in writing or into a tape recorder? If I gave each scar a voice and allowed it to speak, would it have wisdom to offer? It's possible. Decisions were involved. Consequences resulted. Lessons were learned. Since my scars are likely to be my permanent companions, I might do well to let them be my teachers. Maybe my emotional scars also have useful stories to tell.

My scar stories reveal a lot about who I am.

Rules

People expect so much of me: I ought to be around more; I should be willing to sacrifice everything for my loved one; I should do my duty and not feel sorry for myself. They keep coming up with rules that they think I should live by.

There are all kinds of unwritten rules about what a caregiver should do—family rules, community rules, cultural rules. But do they fit my situation? Are they based on values I agree with and find important? Will they serve my interests and my loved one's? Will they do more harm than good? Ultimately, except for legal matters, it's up to me to decide what rules to live by. I know that no matter which rules I choose to follow, I won't satisfy everyone. Before I accept anyone else's rules, I seek guidance from my Spiritual Power and my heart. I also consult wise people I know and assess my own circumstances. Then I trust my inner wisdom and do what seems best.

I follow the rules that seem wise to me.

Self-protection

When my loved one's behavior becomes extreme, I try to ride it out with him. If he gets violent or delusional or suicidal, I muster all my courage and love and try to help him through it. But sometimes it's too much for me. Still, I worry that something terrible will happen if I step back.

But I do have limits. I'm not superhuman and I don't have an answer for every problem. It's all right for me to step back, even before I hit my limit. I do what I can reasonably do, I get what help I can for him, and that's it. Recognizing my limits might mean getting a professional involved. It might mean calling 911. It might mean removing potentially dangerous items from the house. I will take whatever steps I can to keep myself from having to be in a fearful or defensive mode. I can't be the eternal rescuer for others. At times I need to rescue myself.

*I refuse to let the insanity of others endanger me
or drive me insane.*

Saying No

Even though my hands are full, people still ask me to do more. They can't seem to understand how busy I am, how tired I get. I should tell them no, but I don't like to disappoint people. I will say no when I'm angry and at the end of my rope, though usually I make up phony excuses to get out of doing more.

When I have a clear sense of self-respect, I realize that I don't have to say yes to everything people ask me to do. I have a right to choose for myself. I can still be a kind and pleasant person even though I say no. If I keep saying yes, people will keep asking. They won't know I don't want to do something unless I tell them. It's up to me to set the boundaries. I don't have to be mean about it. I can simply show respect for my own needs and preferences by saying, "No, I'm not available for that." In most cases, an explanation is not required. Saying "No" is sufficient.

I choose the activities that are right for me
and my situation.

Unrushed Solutions

In the rush of life, I want things to happen in a hurry. When I see a solution to a problem that concerns my loved one, I push forward to get to it. I tend to get overly impatient and bullish with anyone or anything in my way.

I'm moving so fast that I expect everything to move fast. However, fast isn't always best. Of course, there are moments when immediate action is necessary, but most of the time the pressure to rush is a self-created emergency. When I'm constantly in a hurry, my life becomes a blur. I see only quick, small, band-aid solutions. The core problem keeps festering because I'm not getting to the bottom of the matter. And I'm not open to the kind of creative or unexpected solutions that come to me when I'm in a more relaxed and receptive state. But when I take a breather, step back, and tune in to what's important rather than what's urgent, I have access to bigger and better answers.

I like the taste of slow-cooked wisdom.

My Goals

Because of my caregiving responsibilities, the rest of my life is on hold. I had plans before this all started. I still have changes I'd like to make in my career, home, and family, but what I want has to wait.

Well, maybe not everything. I might not be able to make all the changes I want to make, but I could do a little to move forward with my plans. It's true, most of my time and energy is devoted to caring for my loved one, but nothing says I can't let my mind wander toward my goals when I'm cruising along on the freeway or waiting in line. I could take a tiny step of some kind in the right direction every day, or at least every week. I could make one phone call, jot down a few ideas, or visit a place I need to check out. Inching forward on a regular basis keeps the dream alive and gives me hope. I don't tackle any more than is reasonable in light of my current responsibilities, but I do what I can.

Today I'll take a tiny step toward my goals.

Not Enough Money

The medical bills keep mounting. My income is down. It seems likes I can never keep up, let alone get ahead. I stay awake nights worrying about paying the bills.

When I focus on my money problems, they just seem to get bigger. I think I'll try the opposite for a while. I'll picture myself doing just fine financially. In my mind, I imagine I'm getting everything I need either because I have plenty of money or because good things come to me in some other way. Just imagining myself in better financial shape can help me think about how to move in that direction. Even if big changes don't happen, I'm not really doing all that badly as things stand right now. The basics are taken care of, people are helping out in a number of ways, and I'm smart enough to investigate and take advantage of opportunities when they come up. I'll manage somehow.

If I look around, I'll see that there are many ways
I can get what I need.

Closeness

Since my loved one developed health problems, I've spent a lot of time with him and a lot of time thinking about him. This has become a special opportunity to bring us closer together.

Although I wish he didn't have this health problem, I'm glad it has strengthened our connection. I'm more attentive to him than I would be otherwise. And since he has come to rely on me in a new way, he is more attentive to me. We are partners in this experience, learning a new dance together. And because the steps keep changing, we have to stay in close touch with each other. I listen attentively to his wishes, his struggles, his concerns. He is tuned in to me as well, helping me through these challenging times with his gratitude, encouragement, and respect for my needs.

I treasure our closeness.

Crises

It seems there's a new crisis every time I turn around. A sudden change in my loved one's condition. An accident. A need for hospitalization. I never know what will hit next. I'd like things to calm down for a while.

Sudden changes are harder to take than gradual ones. They require an immediate change of plans and critical decision making. When the adrenaline rush is on, it's hard to think clearly, and rising tension tests everyone's health and patience. What if I developed a plan for crises? Obviously I can't plan for everything. But I can keep emergency phone numbers handy and make arrangements for a friend to give me support in times of crisis. I can also practice staying calm and clearheaded under duress. If I regularly meditate and pray, if I routinely do deep breathing and relaxation exercises, if I rely on my intuition, I will be able to choose more wisely when a sudden change occurs.

I will cultivate a peaceful state of mind today.

Answering Questions

So many people ask me how my loved one is doing. I'm glad they're interested, and yet I tire of reporting on her condition over and over. The information can get quite complicated, and I'm not sure how much detail people really want or need to know. Sometimes I feel pressured to give more information than I want to.

Some people ask about her because they just like to know things. Others are eager to pass the word along. Some ask so they can figure out how to be helpful. But mostly, people want to show they care. That's the main message for me to tune in to. I can show that I appreciate their care, without giving elaborate answers to every question. I do not have to strain to respond to other people's curiosity or idle interest. I save my energy and reduce my frustration if I reply in ways that respect my loved one and myself while still keeping those who need to know appropriately informed.

Not everyone needs to hear the whole story.

Bad Moods

I get in a foul mood sometimes. I feel ornery. Nothing anyone does, myself included, seems right. It's like a dark cloud settles over me and I can't lift it. When I feel like that, I should stay away from people, but I still have my caregiving duties to do.

Luckily, moods pass. That's a good thing to remember when I'm in a bad one. I don't have to let my mood run me and ruin my day. I also don't have to work at changing it. I can stop a moment, take a deep breath, and become an observer of my mood, like a reporter, watching it with interest but not getting caught up in it. By stepping back from it a little, I remove myself from its grip. I am able to see that this mood is a passing storm, and I can wait it out until the sun shines. I avoid making any decisions or judgments in this frame of mind. If a nap or a meal or a good cry is what I need at the moment, I tend to that. The sun often shines a bit sooner when I do.

Bad moods, like dark clouds, move on.

Clarity

I've got such a jumble of thoughts and feelings about all that is happening to my loved one and me. A hundred problems seem to be running through my head at once. I get confused and tired trying to figure out what to do with them all.

When I have too many things to figure out at once, it can help to write them all down. My journal is a private place where I can sort out my problems and my feelings about them. I make a list of the issues on my mind, and one by one, pour all my thoughts and feelings about them onto the journal page. I'm always surprised by how much this helps me clarify what is going on. It's like emptying the contents of my junk drawer on a table. I can sort things out, decide what to keep or toss, and use what I find to make repairs or create next steps.

I'm glad for the clarity my journal writing gives me.

Favorite Places

My loved one and I have some favorite places we have lived or visited. Some we can never visit again together because of his condition. I have photos, I have memories, but I miss these places, especially our times together there.

I'm glad we've had those experiences. I wish we could go to those places again but we can't. I do hold them in my heart and keep their memorabilia at hand. Sometimes I close my eyes and recall how I felt being there and bask in that feeling again. I'd like to find ways to keep this feeling alive in our life together now. We can't go back, but I can look for places that we can go or activities we can do that might remind us of those wonderful places we treasure. My imagination can at least explore that possibility.

Memory, memorabilia, and imagination can help to keep alive the places we have loved together.

Growing Things

I have a hunger for fresh, living things. I grow tired of the stale smells and sounds of sickness that permeate my life. And my loved one's environment has been taken over by lifeless mechanical, pharmaceutical, electronic, and artificial supports. I have to look hard for signs of life!

I get out in nature as much as I can, but I also like to have nature's vibrancy close at hand. My loved one enjoys it too. Pets, with their licking and leaping or swimming or chirping, bring energy into the room and cause smiles. With all their liveliness, they prompt me to forget the limitations imposed by my loved one's condition. Thriving greenery and bright-colored flowers keep me aware of beauty and of the changes that living things go through. I like to let in fresh air whenever possible and allow the outdoor aromas to replace the stagnancy.

Fresh, growing things keep me fresh and growing.

I'm a Fighter

At times my loved one is restricted by rules and regulations. Organizations limit what he can do. So do his own thoughts. My thoughts can limit him, too. I start to think that something is impossible or "shouldn't" be done.

But there are times when something must be done, and I have to find a way no matter what. I get on a mission and I refuse to listen to "you can't" from anyone, even from the negative voices in my own head. I have to fight to get what he needs. If that means setting aside all the rules and regulations for the time being, then so be it. The same goes for any internal resistance—his or mine. I call forth all my courage and determination. I use whatever means are necessary to get done what needs to be done. It may take diplomacy, strength, persistence, and deep love, but if it's right to do it, I do it.

I am a fighter when I need to be.

I Can't Sleep

I don't always sleep well. I stay awake worrying. The least little sound has me wondering what's wrong. My mind races and I can't relax.

Putting my thoughts on paper can be helpful. Sometimes I make a list of what needs to be done and get them off my mind. Or I write pros and cons about a decision I'm trying to make to get a clearer sense of what to do. I write a letter to my Higher Power explaining my plight and asking for help. I put down my honest feelings in all their intensity. I jot down thoughts I want to be rid of and then rip up the piece of paper to show I'm done with them. Writing is a good friend that helps me clear my mind, regain my balance, and feel peaceful. Then I can rest.

I use writing to clarify and ease my thinking and to release stressful emotions.

Heroes

I've read about heroes. I've seen movies about people who triumphed over odds. I wish somebody could be a hero in this situation and rescue my loved one from this agony.

Although I'm not likely to see the carefully scripted heroes of dramatic plots showing up here, I meet real heroes every day. My loved one has made a heroic journey, rising above her condition and beating the odds in all sorts of ways. And many of her caregivers have given heroic service to help her. The heroism I witness isn't the big-screen variety. It's in the little moments when someone demonstrates large love, or risks facing the truth, or brings lightness and laughter into the gloom. Those are the acts of courage I admire. Although no one may be able to reverse my loved one's condition, the heroes around her diminish its effects and create happy endings in the heart that no screen hero can rival.

Heroism is a triumph of the spirit.

I Don't Have to Be in Control

What if something goes wrong? What if one of the doctors makes a mistake? What if I can't get the agency or organization to cooperate? What if somebody doesn't show up who's supposed to? I want everything to go smoothly, to turn out just right. I try so hard, and it seems like things go wrong anyway. I get angry and exhausted trying to set everything straight.

I wonder what would happen if I didn't try so hard to control things. I may be setting myself up for disaster when I try to take charge of everything, when I think I can control whatever happens. Lots of things don't turn out as planned, despite my best efforts. It's a huge burden to take on responsibility for everything turning out all right. Maybe it's a burden I could do without. I could consider it good news that not only do I not control everything, but I don't have to.

I lighten up a little on the controls
and adjust to circumstances as needed.

Holy Moments

Sometimes I step back and look at the person I care for with amazement. In the midst of all the hard stuff that happens—the pain, the disappointments, the losses—there are moments when it's as though a light shines through my loved one. Courage, patience, love, and kindness beam forth as if coming through her from a heavenly source. I am touched.

I'm so glad I'm able to care for this special person in my life, despite how hard it is sometimes. These moments of shining give me a sense of the holy. Times like these I stop and say a prayer of gratitude.

*I take a moment today to experience
the shining presence of my loved one.*

Impossible

My situation seems impossible at times. The living arrangements, the medications, the finances—so many things seem out of hand. I can't see a solution and I'm at my wit's end.

Where can I start to unravel this mess? I guess that even asking the question means I believe there is a place to start. I think I'll start by taking a deep breath or two. What do you know? At least my lungs are working! So, I'll start with what is working. If I stop to notice and appreciate what's going okay, I have a better chance of seeing promise and possibilities in other parts of my life. I know there are answers, and I can find them if I'm willing to let go of "impossible" thinking. Another deep breath. What else can I think of that's going okay right now?

> *I slow down and jot down what is working*
> *and build solutions from there.*

Heart Messages

I've heard there are things you ought to say to a loved one who is seriously ill, things about the meaning of your relationship. You should try to clear up old hurts. But I don't know how to bring up those subjects, and I'm not sure he'll want to talk about them.

What I want to do is to say what's in my heart. But trying to make myself talk to him because I "should" won't work. Perhaps it's enough to go to him with a sincere intention to deliver my heart's message and to listen to what's in his. That way I can remain present and open with him without feeling any pressure to say the right thing. When the time is right I'll say what I need to say, or he'll speak up. The timing of the heart can never be forced. It may come in words or a tender touch or a tear. I can't predict or plan exactly how, but I can trust my heart to express love, and that's all that matters.

The message of an open heart cannot be held back.

The Insensitivity of Others

The way some people treat my loved one disturbs me. Their faces show pity or disgust or annoyance. They talk in patronizing ways. They ignore him and talk past him. I get angry. I can tell he feels hurt. I feel caught in the middle.

I know I can't control what other people say or do, so I do what I can to minimize the effects of their hurtful, demeaning treatment. I talk to my loved one about what happened and show compassion. I don't take others' insensitive behavior personally. Their actions are not a reflection of my loved one's worth, or mine. They may not know how to be compassionate. Sometimes I ask people, in a respectful way, to act differently. I suggest that they speak directly and genuinely to my loved one, and I demonstrate what I mean. If people continue to be insensitive, I do what I can to avoid contact with them in the future.

My loved one deserves respect,
and I will help him get it.

Money Decisions

My loved one's care is costing a lot of money. I wish that money didn't have to be spent this way. She had other plans for it and so did I.

I never thought the money being spent on her care would become a big issue for me. But if I'm honest with myself, I resent losing some of the financial security and opportunities which that money would have provided. I have to admit that my decisions about her care tend to get colored by these feelings. So when I'm involved in a money decision, it helps if I stop to check my own motivation: Am I keeping her interests and mine in proper balance? Am I being fair to others who are being affected? Am I expecting others to pick up the tab for my loved one's care? I weigh these questions against my values, and I do my best to maintain my integrity.

*I bring my choices about money in line
with my values.*

People Criticize

I'm doing the best job I can taking care of my loved one, but I get a lot of static from some people. They don't like how I'm doing things. They think his condition is my fault. Or they think I'm in this for the money. It hurts me and it makes me mad.

I tend to take their comments personally. But it helps to remember that what they say is a reflection of their own hurt and fear, their own sadness and confusion. I am not "wrong" and neither are they. We are all doing what makes the most sense to us based on what we've learned in life. No one is perfect. I don't want to drain my energy obsessing about their criticism. I've got other options. I can use my imagination to put up a mental shield that deflects their anger right back to them. I can walk away. I can thank them for their concerns and tell them I respect their preferences, but say that I am making a different choice. I can pray for them.

*I will make a list of my options for responding
to criticism and use them as needed.*

Receiving

I am so touched when my loved one says things to cheer me up or is kind in other ways. I feel a little awkward though, guilty almost. I am the one who is supposed to be cheerful and kind. I shouldn't expect to get such thoughtful support from someone who is suffering.

Then again, I don't know why the giving should be all in one direction. It's not as if a person who is ill or disabled has nothing left to give. Even the most infirm person has a heart. In fact, I'm sure it must be difficult for my loved one to be unable to give in the ways she always has in the past. Every person wants to have value, to have something to offer. If at times all my loved one can do is smile, tell a joke, or say a pleasant word, that is her full capacity to give at that moment. When she gives me these things, they are truly a gift of her whole self. I would be foolish not to accept such a gift.

I give and I receive with a grateful heart.

Leaving Things Behind

My heart breaks when my loved one has to leave one more precious thing behind. Moving from a cherished home, selling off belongings, or simply giving up some special item that she can no longer keep or use—any of these can seem like an amputation, a loss that can never be replaced.

I can only watch and show I care. I cannot replace the loss. I cannot take away the pain. I feel at a loss myself, a witness with no remedy to offer. Perhaps being an attentive, caring witness is the best thing I can be at that moment. Just standing empty alongside my loved one as she goes through her emptying, is a gift to her. There is something sacred about standing side by side with someone at a time of loss. The emptiness is not held alone.

> *I am willing to feel the emptiness of loss*
> *alongside my loved one.*

Quality of Life

It would be nice if my loved one could always be in her own home or stay with someone in the family. I keep wondering if there is more I could do to make that possible.

I am tempted to think that, if only I were willing to make a few more sacrifices, she would never have to be in someone else's care. But I know she needs things at times that I cannot provide. I can't control that. What I can do, though, is to find little ways to contribute to her quality of life when she is in someone else's care. I can bring her things she enjoys, I can spend unhurried time with her, I can provide some decorative touches for her room. Whatever I can do for her, I do gladly. It doesn't help to waste time on wishful thinking. Instead, I use my creative skills to add whatever comforts, pleasures, and beauty I can to her present environment, wherever it is.

I contribute creatively to my loved one's quality of life.

Regrets

I look back on some things I have done while caring for my loved one and realize that I should not have done them. I didn't realize at the time that they would cause so much damage.

It's true there are times when I'm not at my best. Sometimes I do things that create serious problems. When my actions involve my loved one, who has no choice but to depend on me, I feel especially responsible and it's easy to punish myself for years to come. I tend to think that if I feel guilty enough and am harsh enough with myself, I can make up for my damaging actions. I can't. It doesn't help the person I am caring for and it doesn't help me. What does help is to admit what I did, apologize if possible, do what I can to correct the situation, and then forgive myself. Then I can lay the past to rest.

Today I set things right and set myself free.

Rhymes for the Times

When I'm overtired from all my caregiving responsibilities, I either get crabby or silly. Silly feels better. I ought to go for silly more often...even when I'm not overtired.

Rhymes can be ridiculous. Maybe they're a good place to start. I can write a bunch of them, use them to make up songs, and get others to add onto them. They don't even have to make sense. "Being ill is a pill, not a thrill; I've had my fill of this drill." "A fat cat went to bat, fell flat, and went splat on a hat." "No meds on this bed. I'm wearing red Keds as I head for the Feds to get me out of here."

There's no time to rhyme like the present.

Unfairness

Not everyone involved in my loved one's care has her best interests in mind. This is a time for support and understanding, but some people are insensitive or selfish. Their neglect or manipulation of my loved one add insult to injury. I do what I can to protect her, but I can't always put a stop to their actions. And I often end up being treated like the bad guy. That's unfair.

I could become bitter and vengeful over this unfairness, but I would only make myself more miserable. It helps if I reassure myself that I am doing the best I can to make things right for my loved one. It also helps to talk about my frustration with my friends or the members of my support group. Then I am reminded that I'm not the only one who has to deal with unfairness, and I find the strength to prevent the disturbing actions of others from dragging me down.

*I hang onto my peace of mind
even when life is unfair.*

Transitions

I've had to make many adjustments since I've been caregiving. New schedules, new expectations, new relationships—I've found a way to work them all into my life. But just when I've settled into these new routines, along comes another change to wrench away the now familiar patterns and demand yet another round of adjustments.

I realize that the only real norm is change. Yet each new procedure or activity—once I get used to it—becomes "mine." When I'm asked to give it up, I resist, at least momentarily. It's my "security blanket." I want to be flexible and ready to adapt to changing needs, yet it's important to be patient with my natural desire for the familiar. When it's time to give up a person or activity I've grown used to, it helps to find extra ways to comfort myself during the transition. I snuggle up with my pet, chat with an understanding friend, or buy myself flowers.

I make sure my sense of security is well tended to during times of transition.

Touch

People are afraid to touch my loved one. They're either afraid they might "catch" what she's got, or they're afraid they might hurt or offend her somehow. Yet she would welcome their reassuring touch. And I'd welcome a comforting hug myself.

I realize that people have mixed feelings about touching someone. But they might be willing to offer the comfort of their touch if they knew how helpful it would be. With some people I am able to ask directly for a hug or a shoulder rub or a foot massage for me or my loved one. With others, it works better to combine my request for touch with a practical task. I ask them to comb my loved one's hair or apply her sunscreen. Or I ask them to assist with putting on her shoes, jacket, or gloves. Always I remember that touch is a form of tender communion between two people. I make sure my loved one's preferences and mine regarding touch are respected.

I invite and receive touch respectfully.

Values

I have many decisions to make every day about my loved one's care. I often wonder if I'm making the right choices.

I remember somebody telling me that "the most important thing is to keep the most important thing the most important thing." With so many decisions to make, it's easy for me to forget what's most important. Usually, whatever is in front of me seems most important at that moment. But it might only be the noisiest or messiest thing. I could help myself remember what's most important by making a list of my values. What would I put on such a list? Family loyalty? Love? Spiritual beliefs? Independence? Once I'm clear about my values, I could assign them each a priority. Which are truly the most important? The less important? By sorting out my values, I can better determine where to direct my time and attention. And my daily decisions will match my values and priorities.

I know what my values are and I live by them.

The Strength for Today

A lot of days I wonder if I can make it until bed-time. I have to do things that seem far beyond what's possible for me. I get so worn out and feel so sad. I can't imagine how I'm going to hold on for the days and weeks and maybe years ahead.

On days like this, the only way I know if I'm going to get through the day is when the end of the day comes. As I get ready for bed, I say to myself, "I got through another one." Then I'm so fatigued I drop into bed. But I got through it. That's the important thing. I got through it! Even on days when the impossible is demanded of me, somehow I make it through. Knowing that gives me strength. The days and weeks ahead may be tough, but one day at a time I can get through them.

I've got the strength to get through today.

Decisions I Disagree With

I don't always agree with the decisions my loved one and others around him make. I can see a better course of action. Sometimes decisions don't get made at all, and I feel an urgency to get things handled. My patience is tested.

Even though I think I know what's best for others, people have the right to make their own choices about their lives as long as they are mentally competent. My job is to communicate my wishes and feelings respectfully. But it's also a good idea to let others know what I intend to do if they make certain decisions. Then—and this is sometimes the hard part—I let go of my need to be "right"; I respect others' wisdom about their own destiny. If I have made my position clear and the decisions don't suit me, I maintain integrity by following through on what I said I would do.

I communicate my preferences clearly and respectfully, and then let go of the outcome.

Acceptance

I have this fantasy that I'll wake up one morning and my loved one will be in perfect health. All his problems will be gone. This nightmare will be over. I have this fantasy because I don't want to accept that he'll never be perfectly well again.

I know I'm being unrealistic. Sure, there may be improvements, but everything will not change overnight. They may never change. But I manage better if I face this reality in small doses. I can't handle it all at once. Maybe having the fantasy is all right once in a while; it helps me ease into acceptance and feels better than imagining the worst. That image throws me into deep sorrow. Another option is to compromise—imagining the best coming out of even the worst possible scenarios. Or I can conceive of a continuum—imagining a range of outcomes and then adjusting to meet each situation as it comes up.

> *I can accept what is happening*
> *when I know I have choices.*

Amazing Accomplishments

Taking care of someone else has been one of the toughest things I've ever done. I've had to make some very difficult decisions, and, while I haven't done everything perfectly, I've managed pretty well. Some of my efforts you could almost call heroic. I feel good about what I've done and I don't want to forget my accomplishments on darker days.

It might be a good idea to take time every day to make note of how well I've done. I could finish my day by inventorying what I am pleased about and relishing the satisfaction that goes with it. I could also identify those things I'm less pleased about and then gently forgive myself and others. If any damage has been done, I can make a plan to set things right. That way I'm able to feel complete with my day, and rest well. When dark days come, I can look back on my writing to remember that I've done many things well and overcome many difficulties.

Despite my difficulties, I have triumphed.

Breaking Promises

I have made promises to myself and to my loved one that I can't keep, and that is very painful for me. I want to stay true to my word, but circumstances have changed and now I can't do what I promised. I feel so guilty.

I was sincere when I made my promise. I made them out of love, with the best interest of my loved one in mind. But I could not anticipate some of the changes that have come along since. My promises were based on what I knew when I made them. I lived up to them as long as they made sense. But I would be foolish now to continue carrying them out when they would do more harm than good. More important than promises is following the spirit behind those promises—doing what's loving and best for my loved one's health and sanity. I can make such a choice in peace.

I am faithful to the spirit of my promises,
even if I can't carry them out exactly as planned.

Depression

I notice my loved one gets discouraged at times. She becomes lethargic, doesn't seem to care about her recovery. She acts helpless. I get angry that she seems to have given up. I can't help her if she won't help herself.

This behavior does not seem like her. I tend to think she's just being stubborn, but perhaps she is depressed. I know that some health problems can lead to changes in the brain that affect mood. Or it's possible that her lack of interest and energy is a cover for the deep grief she is feeling about all her losses. Medications can also affect mood. Whatever the cause, she may not be able to get out of this dark emotional state of by herself. Trying to cheer her up doesn't seem to work. She may benefit from being checked for depression. Perhaps the doctor can recommend some solutions.

I'm attentive to my loved one's moods and take steps to get her help when she needs it.

Willing to Make Changes

I don't always like how I'm handling things. I try to change, and I make progress for a little while, but then I slip right back into the old way of doing things. It's easy to get discouraged.

I know that if I want to change, I have to sincerely want to let go of the old ways. That means giving up the benefits I've been reaping from the old behavior. As people who overspend get "high" from shopping (even though they don't like paying the bills later), I get something out of my old ways of behaving. Maybe the rebel in me likes the feeling of independence I get from my actions, or maybe I get to feel righteous about what I do. If I take a few moments to list the benefits I get from the behaviors I want to change, I get clear about what I will be giving up. Then I can gently acknowledge the loss, be patient with myself, and ask my Spiritual Power for guidance in making the changes.

I am willing to do what it takes
to behave the way I want to.

Fear

When my loved one's condition worsens or a new test is done or a new treatment tried, it's easy to get scared. I fear the results and tend to expect the worst. And the more I dwell on disasters that could happen, the more the fear seems to grow.

In a way, fear is contagious. My loved one picks up on it and so do other people around me. The tension mounts. So, when I start to feel fear, I can't let it take over. If fear bursts in on me, I leave the room and find a way to release it. I might have to feel the fear in a big way before I can let it go. But then I have a talk with my fear and tell it that it's not helpful now and that I'm going to send it away. I let my Spiritual Power take charge of my fear. After that I am firm about shifting my attention away from fearful thoughts to calming and positive ones.

Fear leaves me when I trust in my Spiritual Power.

Food Help

Cooking can be quite a chore since the person I'm caring for has different food needs than I do. I don't like to have to cook more than one meal, so I end up getting take-out food for myself or nibbling on odds and ends. I never feel satisfied. It takes a lot of work to eat right and I don't have the energy for it.

Perhaps this is one of those things people could do for me who want to help. I could ask a few different people to bring over a meal once in a while, maybe even regularly. That would help out so much and might also let me visit with them if I'm in the mood. I could even give them a few ideas about favorite foods I especially enjoy. It would feel so good to have somebody look out for me a little.

I can ask others to show their concern in practical ways that help me stay healthy and happy.

Intolerance

I've been known to run out of patience. When I don't like the way things are done, I can get indignant and start demanding answers. People either respond by trying to appease me or they get defensive and angry. Things usually escalate until nobody is happy.

I want to have respectful, cooperative relationships with people but my intolerance creates alienation and resentment. I might get what I demand, but I don't get what I really want. It might help to do a little "soul-searching"—to look for the core soul in others. Underneath everyone's behavior is a radiant, spiritual center. If I'm willing to see the light shining through someone, it is there. My intolerance clouds the view. But I can close my eyes and imagine that light coming through the heart of the person I'm upset with and joining with my light to put my problem situation in a "better light."

Standing in the shining light of another's soul removes my intolerance.

New Activities

I've got new routines since I've been caring for my loved one—specific things that she especially enjoys. I enjoy doing them, too, because they make life a little more pleasant for her. I've had to give up some other things I like to do; these new activities have become more important. I'm thankful I can do them.

I'm surprised how I've taken up these activities that I never could have imagined doing before. I'm glad to discover my own flexibility and generosity. By giving the gift of time and attention to my loved one, I'm learning more about what I'm capable of giving. And what seemed like a sacrifice at first has become something I now look forward to. Caregiving is giving me many new ways to expand what I know, what I can do, and what I enjoy.

I'm glad I can give to my loved one,
and I'm glad for the gifts I receive when I do.

Gratitude

On days when I can't come up with a positive thought, I need a way to lift myself up. When my thinking goes sour, I'm not much good for myself, let alone for my loved one. I need a day brightener.

When I'm in that state of mind, I try to think of something to be grateful for. That's almost guaranteed to get me started back in an upward direction. I may have to look hard at first and start with something basic like, "I'm grateful I am able to move today," or "I'm grateful my eyes and hands work." It helps especially if I write them down. Once I get a couple of items on my gratitude list, I can come up with more. Pretty soon, the scale starts to tip toward recognizing how much good is going on in my life, and I get back in balance. There's more sweet than sour.

> *A gratitude list helps me remember*
> *what is going well in my life.*

Time for Myself

I never seem to have any time anymore. All the things I have to do for my loved one keep me so busy, I don't get to do things I want to do. I barely find time to get a haircut or get groceries. I almost never go out and have fun. I want some time just for me.

Taking time for myself isn't as easy as it once was, but it's still possible if I plan ahead a little. Can I get someone to fill in for me once in a while so I can get away or have a few hours alone? Can I schedule an activity for myself when my loved one is resting? Can I invite someone over for a game of cards, a cup of coffee, or a time of prayer together? It's important to take a few minutes at least once a day to get off by myself to do something I enjoy, even if it means shutting myself in the bathroom to do it.

I deserve to have time for myself,
and I intend to take it.

Over-Concern, Over-Control

I've tried to find the ideal arrangements for my loved one. I've sought the best care with the best people possible. Yet, the organizations providing her care are flawed. I don't understand why I can't get everything my loved one needs.

Of course, there is no perfect solution. Every system and every person has faults. It helps if I realize I've made a good choice and accept the people and systems for what they are. While I will always advocate for the best possible care, I can't expect complete compliance all the time. Maybe I'm a bit overly concerned. I feel so frustrated about my inability to control my loved one's condition that I try to control all the circumstances surrounding her. It would be more honest to admit my own disappointment over her condition. Then I can more easily accept those aspects of her condition that won't change no matter how well she is taken care of.

I let go of my desires to have more control
than is possible.

I'm Not Responsible for Everything

Sometimes I agonize over something that went wrong while I was away. I think: I should have been there. If I had been, things would have turned out better. It's my fault. I can't help feeling responsible for the way things have turned out.

I care so much. I want to do the right things for my loved one who is so precious to me. If I'm not on top of everything every minute, I feel like I'm responsible if something goes wrong. But it's foolish to think I can be everywhere at all times and always make the right decisions. That's impossible. And even if I am present, things can still go wrong. I don't have control over how everything turns out. Silly me: I must think I have much more power than I do. Since when is everything that goes wrong my fault?

I'll only take responsibility for doing the best I can.

Little Things

It's the accumulation of little things that gets to me. The medicine bottle that won't open, or spills when you do open it. Someone moving too slow. Losing track of paperwork. A few of these little things in a day, and I begin to lose my patience. When that happens, it feels like the whole world is against me and nothing will ever work right. It's all I can do to maintain control.

And yet I know that each of these things is little by itself. The trick is to put the thing immediately into perspective so it stays little. A phrase to say to myself as soon as each new irritation arises is "No big deal." Not that I want to ignore my immediate feeling of irritation, but, by taking a deep breath and remembering to say "No big deal," I help to expand my awareness beyond that immediate situation. In the long run, very few things are a big deal. When I remind myself of that truth, I keep unnecessary pressure from building up.

Little things are little things.

My Calling

My God, how can I do this? Yet how can I not do this? I don't know how I'll manage it, I just know it must be done by somebody. If not me, who? But I feel so unprepared, so frightened.

Whether I like it or not, the challenge of my loved one's care is in front of me. I am as prepared as I'm going to be. I may not have time to even blink for the duration. So I won't blink. I won't hesitate. If it's here for me to do, I'll do it. I'm the one who's right for the job because it's mine to do. I have what I need—my willingness and my presence. It's like a calling that has my name on it. Knowing that the strength of my Spiritual Power will carry me through, I'll answer yes. My loved one needs all I've got, so here goes.

If it's mine to do, I'll do it.

Pleasure

One moment of pleasure would seem like a pot of gold right now. But pleasure seems as remote as finding gold. My love one's difficulties are multiplied by the huge toll her care is taking on me. I forget what pleasure feels like.

What in my life could possibly give me pleasure? When I'm in such a drab state of mind, I have trouble imagining something pleasant. Funny, when I was a kid I never had trouble with that. Crayon in hand, I could make a shining sun or happy face. I could sing a nursery rhyme and feel glad. I could see a picture in a magazine and right away imagine myself in that picture enjoying myself. Maybe I could pull out a crayon right now to help me remember what pleasure is. Perhaps humming a simple, familiar melody or writing a funny rhyme might wake up those good feelings I long for. Who knows? That pot of gold might start to materialize.

Pleasure is at hand if I'm willing to play along.

Role Shifts

I'm not always sure how to relate to my loved one. I want to be with her in all the familiar ways we've enjoyed for a long time. Yet I now have these new ways of caring for her that don't fit well with that traditional role.

It's so easy to slip into the caregiving role when that's not what's called for. Because I care so much, I tend to do more than she needs done. Other times I tend to expect her to be her old familiar self and I resent having to do the extra things for her that she can no longer do on her own. If I don't pay attention, the boundaries between roles become slippery. It helps if I pause to think: Is this activity hers or mine to do? Is it part of my caregiving responsibilities or is this something that fits within our broader relationship? Sometimes the two roles overlap, and that's okay too. Flexibility, attention, and respect are all called for to maintain balance.

I stay aware of my roles as they vary
throughout the day.

Valuing Myself

Some days I feel like all I am is an errand-runner, and not a very good one at that. I get a lot of things wrong. I can't keep up with all the chores and everything else people want from me. I feel like I'm in over my head and start to give up on myself.

On days like that, I do whatever I can to boost my spirits. I have to feel good about myself or I'm likely to go under. I ask others around me to give me a boost. If I'm alone, I take other steps to restore my sense of self-worth and confidence: I listen to uplifting music. I sing songs that declare my strength. I wear shirts with sayings on them that remind me I'm worthwhile and capable. I put my arms around myself and give myself a hug. I take a deep breath and draw on my Spiritual Power. I buy myself a treat. I look in the mirror and smile at myself and tell myself I'm doing a fine job.

I am my own cheerleader.

Rules of the System

Whether I'm dealing with a health care system, government agencies, or social services, there are always rules that seem to hinder more than help. I get so frustrated.

Some rules are necessary to keep order, protect people, and control costs. But I wish they could be bent when it's common sense to do so. Because of the stress I'm feeling, I'm very impatient with all the paperwork and bureaucracy. I'm sure others become impatient with me, too, when I pressure them to do things my way. I need to find a balance between being reasonably patient with the rules of large, complex systems and being reasonably impatient when those rules don't make sense. I know I can be stronger and more effective when I'm calm and diplomatic. I will check in with my Spiritual Power for wisdom, strength, and peacefulness as I assess the situation and ask for what I want.

*I treat others with high regard as I ask them
to be responsive.*

Planning

I would like to talk with my loved one about what will happen as his health deteriorates. As he loses certain abilities, we'll have to make decisions about everything from living arrangements to perhaps legal guardianship, but I don't know how to bring up these matters with him.

I know it's hard for him to face the inevitable changes coming. It's hard for me too. Yet I want to avoid the consequences if we don't deal with these matters now while he's still able to. I could sit down with him and ask him to do me a favor. Then I could say, "I'd like you to think about what might happen if…." He may find the subject too unsettling to talk about at first so I won't push it, but I can try again later. I can tell him I realize how hard these matters are to talk about but that his opinions and decisions are important to me.

*I want help in making plans
and I ask for it clearly and compassionately.*

Love through the Losses

I watch my loved one and see the person before me diminishing. Her old abilities are gone. Her interests are not as strong. It's much harder to have a conversation with her now. So much has been lost.

Sadness creeps up on me. I want so much to have back the person I once knew. I miss all the activities, the liveliness, the good times we had together. Even their memory is starting to fade. I know she's never going to be the same and my heart suffers such grief. The loss is huge. I'll let the sadness be here. I'll remember it comes to me because of the deep love I've long had for this very precious person in my life. I'll keep that love alive, and I'll continue to cherish her, even though many things have changed.

All is not lost. Love still lives.

AUGUST 28

Health Regimens

I wish my loved one would do all the things he's supposed to do. There are treatments and medications and activities he needs to tend to, but he forgets or neglects them. I worry about him getting worse.

I realize he's not operating at a hundred percent. It makes sense that his memory or discipline are not all they could be. It helps if I give him instructions in small doses. I also write them down for him and put them where he can see them. When necessary, I give him gentle reminders. I do whatever I can to support him, but I also remember that he is free to make some choices for himself. In most cases, I can't make him do what he is unwilling to do. But my job is to offer support in loving ways, not to control his behavior.

I support my loved one's health regimens
with love and detachment.

Growth

My experience as a caregiver has made me a better person. I didn't think it would turn out that way. I thought it would destroy me. But I have grown in ways that no one can take from me.

I have been hit by challenge after challenge. And they have forced me to dig down deep inside myself to find the strength and resilience and patience I didn't know I had. I have also acquired new skills, and old ones have been seasoned. My faith in my Spiritual Power, in myself, and in other people has been tested. But I have discovered where I stand with each of them, at least for now. Of course, I know the tests aren't over, but I'm stronger now. It might be useful to make a drawing or painting, a collage or carving of all the ways I've grown, using symbols such as animals to represent them. Leaving my creation out on display can serve to remind me on days when I forget how far I've come.

I celebrate my growth.

Keeping Busy

If I sat around every day thinking about the problems I have as a caregiver, I'd have some mighty miserable days. It's better to keep busy. That way, I keep my mind on other things and don't let the ups and downs of caregiving throw me off.

I'm glad I've got my work or other projects or people to occupy me some of the time. Not that I want to ignore my loved one's situation, but I can't focus every waking moment on him. I need the balance of other activities. When I have productive and pleasant experiences away from him, I keep my sanity and come back to him refreshed. Being busy keeps me from worrying too much. Of course, I don't want to "hide out" in my busyness and ignore my feelings about his situation. But it's important to balance attention to my feelings with other activities I find satisfying and stimulating.

I keep active in ways that satisfy me.

The Answer Is "No"

I give lots of time and attention to my loved one who is in need of extra care right now. My heart feels for her. But she is not the only one who wants my attention. Others in the family, at work, and in the community all want something from me. They know I'm a soft touch, and I can't help myself, I keep saying yes. I get exhausted and depressed and there is nothing left for me.

"No" is such a foreign word. My heart wants to say yes and I feel guilty when I say no. But if I want to stop scattering myself in so many directions, I have to learn to say no. And I don't have to give explanations or apologies. No is a fine answer all by itself. "No, I won't be able to do that." "No, but I'm sure you'll find someone else." "No, not this week." By saying no, I'm choosing where to give my time and attention, rather than letting others choose for me.

Saying no allows me to say yes
to what is most important to me.

The Recipe

I want a recipe for how to be a good caregiver. Four parts of this and six parts of that. It would be easier that way. If I could just follow a recipe, I'd get it perfect every day.

So far I haven't been able to find such a recipe. There are lots of clichéd slogans about keeping my chin up and being patient, but it's not that simple. The closest I can come to a prescribed answer is the old grandmother's recipe: a little bit of this and a little bit of that "until it looks right." That's some relief, actually. Since there's no recipe, I've got the freedom to experiment with what seems most reasonable and attractive. All good cooks experiment. I get to try something and see how it turns out. And then if I don't like what happens, next time I can modify the process for a different result. Maybe that's the real recipe.

> *Caregiving is a continual experiment*
> *in creative living.*

Adjustments

I get excited when I figure out how to solve a bothersome problem. Once I get it handled and hit my stride, my life feels in balance and I'm able to relax. But that never lasts. Something new always shows up, demanding yet another adjustment. This is wearing on me.

Caregiving is a lot like skiing or riding a bike. I'm always adjusting to stay balanced and keep on course. I have to be wide awake and keep my whole being flowing with the terrain or I'll go down in a hurry. Even when I've got a long way to go and feel like I'm wearing out, the need for balance and awareness continues. With practice, I learn how to manage my energy, stopping for rests or pushing on as appropriate. I'd like caregiving to be easier, but I'm glad I've found ways to stay flexible and become skilled enough to maneuver a rather bumpy ride.

A long ride over rough terrain can be an adventure.

A Work of Art

I sit and look at my loved one and my heart warms. We've gone through so much together. I treasure the tender appreciation we have for each other. I feel such love.

Our love has been seasoned over time. We've had to get used to the changes in our relationship as her problems have progressed and I've become the caregiver. This wasn't what we expected. Our love and our resilience have been tested on every level and we have some scars to show for it. Yet, we're here, still together, still trying to find our way each day to make things go as well as possible. We're like a sculpture slowly being shaped by our experience. It is made of clay that hasn't hardened yet, so we're still a work in progress.

Together my loved one and I create
a beautiful work of art.

The Power of a Word

I have so many things to do today, I wonder if I'll ever get them done. I have to do chores around the house, run errands, meet people, do a host of things for my loved one. It all feels like too much!

One word could change my day. Like the word "have" in "have to." When I say I "have" to do something, it can seem like a drag. I feel obligated, burdened. What if I said "choose to" or "want to" or "plan to" instead? All of those words put me in charge and lift the sense of burden. "Have to" falsely implies I'm being forced. I'm choosing each action based on what I value, maybe out of love for my dear one or because I want to ease suffering or minimize costs. I do household chores because I value cleanliness and orderliness. I run errands because of what they help me accomplish. Remembering that I'm choosing each activity, and why I'm choosing it, puts me in a positive frame of mind as I approach my day.

How I say things has power.

Uncertainty and Balance

I get weary from the constant changes and uncertainty about my loved one's health and circumstances. Symptoms come and go. Treatments change. New people become involved in the care. I wish things could settle into a routine for a while so I knew what to expect.

There's a balance I'm seeking. When things get too routine in my life, I get bored. When they change all the time, I wish for routine. Balance is not static. Like being on a teeter-totter, it involves a tendency to tip at all times. Yet if I maintain my internal sense of balance, I can adjust to minimize the shock of change. Keeping myself in balance is both an inside and an outside job. To offset the changes in my loved one's situation, I look for ways to stabilize and simplify the rest of my life. To keep my internal sense of balance tuned up, I nap when I'm overtired and do something calming when I'm too keyed up.

I stay in balance to ride out the waves of change.

Vocal Release

I try so hard to be a kind and conscientious caregiver, but all the pressures can get to me. Sometimes I feel like a volcano ready to blow its top. I feel tight, pinched, squeezed, trapped—I can't stand it anymore. I feel like I have to let loose somehow, but I don't want to hurt anyone.

Fortunately, I can blow off steam in the car or in an isolated room or outdoor getaway where no one can hear me. When I'm safely away by myself, I give my vocal chords some exercise. I yell, scream, chant, roar, hiss, moan, cry, or make any other sound that expresses what I can't exactly say with language. I suppose someone might think I'm crazy, but it doesn't matter. No one is around, I know what feels good, and I let that pent-up energy make noise until I've got it all out of my system. Afterwards, my body feels both calm and energized. I might end up by singing or humming on the way back home.

I give my voice full permission to have its say.

Volunteering

When I visit my loved one or take him for treatment, I see how many other people are suffering with debilitating conditions. I get sad and I want to help them all.

Seeing so much suffering almost immobilizes me. I don't know where to start. I haven't got enough energy to help everyone. But I listen to my compassionate heart and do what I can. I start by helping my loved one as much as possible. If I have more time or inclination, I choose a few ways to help others. By volunteering with the organizations that serve my loved one, I make life better for him and for many other people as well. Even if I volunteer for another organization, I am contributing to the circle of care among all people. That will ultimately come back to help us both.

By giving to one, I'm giving to all.

Unpleasant Chores

Some of the things I have to do for my loved one are so unpleasant. I can't stand the thought of having to do them over and over for who knows how long. No "positive attitude" will make them any less desirable. I feel like all I can do is endure.

The hardest part is thinking about having to do them over and over again. So, if thinking about them is the hardest part, perhaps I can change my thinking. I can focus on what I have to do today. While highly unpleasant, today's chores are manageable. And today's chores are the only ones I actually have to be concerned about. I can't do tomorrow's chores today, so why spend energy worrying about them? I'll just do what's in front of me and take the pressure off myself about the future.

I can do what I have to do today.

Changed Appearances

It's not always a pretty sight when I look at my loved one. Her skin sags, her hair is messy, her clothes hang funny, her weight has changed, and her face looks different somehow. Sometimes I hardly recognize this person I've been close to for so long.

It's a shock, really. I hate to admit it, but it is. I have to get used to it, to look for the beauty in this new form. The old appearance may never return. I cry sometimes when I realize that. I miss the old look. It's taking some adjustment on my part to accept the new and all that it means. I will be patient with myself through this change. I will not expect myself to accept it instantly. I will stay in touch with the love that gently helps me see beyond appearances.

I am patient with myself as I face each new change.

Spiritual Companionship

I wish I had somebody to talk to every day about what I'm experiencing. I need to be able to vent my frustrations when my loved one won't cooperate or when the medications cause side effects. I want someone to share the relief with me when the pain subsides or when I figure out how to get some services that my loved one needs. It's those little things I need to tell someone.

I'm glad I have a Spiritual Power to rely on for companionship. I can talk on and on about my day's events, and I know I'll be fully understood and supported. Some days I am so busy talking to the One who guides me that you might say I am always praying. I don't know how I'd survive without being able to do that. I know that nothing I say will be "wrong" or misinterpreted. I'll get complete, loving attention. It's such a relief to know I have a constant companion who will never fail me. I am not alone.

My Spiritual Power is my constant, caring companion.

Taking Charge

When I've had to take charge of some areas of my loved one's life, he doesn't want to let go, even when he can't manage anymore. He's used to being in charge. Sometimes I have to be strong and insist.

I can understand why he wants to maintain control, but it's not feasible now. When he resists, I tend to back off, not wanting to hurt his feelings or to argue with him. But then matters don't get handled that need handling. Problems mount and I worry. I know he'll never be able to take care of these matters himself and eventually I'll have to do them. I'll also have to clean up all the problems that pile up in the meantime. As hard as it might be, if it's time I take charge, it's time. I will set the limits and tell him so. I can ask friends or professionals for encouragement and support, but I will be the one to do it. If I don't, the long-term cost is too high. He might be upset at first, but I trust that he will adjust in time.

I take charge of what I need to take charge of.

The Acts of Strangers

When we're out and about, people stare, ask impolite questions, offer unwanted advice. I wish they'd leave us alone. Sometimes I get so mad I just want to tell them where to go jump off.

I know they usually don't mean harm. They're reacting from shock or curiosity or a desire to help. It helps if I remember that I don't have to accept what they give me any more than I have to buy what a commercial or billboard is selling. If people are being downright rude or mean, I can ignore them or ask them to stop. If I'm not in the mood to answer questions or listen to advice, I can say so in a respectful way or change the subject. If I do end up talking with them, I can teach them about my loved one's condition. I can also listen for any good ideas that might come through in their comments. What I don't like, I can discard.

I am not at the mercy of strangers.

Vulnerability

When I see my loved one's vulnerability, I feel my own. I wonder what might happen to me some day. I wonder if I'll be able to handle it. I am struck by the uncertainty of life and the certainty of death.

I know my time will come. I am frightened. I want to turn away. It hurts to be this close to my own mortality. I allow all these feelings to surface. I face them and know that loss and death are a certain part of my existence as a human being. My loved one's experience is a reminder and an invitation for reflection. This may be a good time to spend a quiet period writing, praying, meditating, or talking with someone close to me. Being fearful of what I might lose may help me look at my life with new eyes. What matters most may become clearer. I allow my Spiritual Power to direct me and strengthen me so I can live each day to the fullest.

I treasure my life and make the most of it.

Creating a Record

This time I spend caring for my loved one is precious. I'm learning so much and having experiences of the heart that I don't want to forget. It seems as though these are times worth recording in some way so I can hang on to all their richness.

Photos and videos may help me remember what we all looked like, but I could also find a way to record my internal impressions of what this caregiving experience has been like for me. I could write poems, reflections, or stories about the intense love, fear, hope, discouragement, pain, and joy I experience. I could make a drawing, painting, collage, banner, carving, or other handwork that symbolizes what this time in my life means to me. The creation will not only give me a record I can treasure for years to come, it will help me find greater understanding and more meaning in what I'm going through now.

Today I will start keeping a record
of my caregiving experience.

Doing Enough

No matter how many things I do for my loved one, I think it's never enough. Surely I could do something else that would relieve the discomfort and make things better. If only I knew more, were stronger, had more time or money....

It's true, there is always something more that I could do, and yet nothing will completely change my loved one's situation for the better. I waste precious energy stewing over what I'm not doing. Of course, I keep looking for ways to improve things, but I am being cruel if I judge myself harshly for not doing things perfectly. I make myself suffer needlessly. In each situation, all I can do is choose what seems the most reasonable and loving thing to do and then do it. That is enough. If my choice doesn't work out well, I can choose differently the next time.

What I do in each moment is enough.

Educating Others

Friends, family, and caring strangers sometimes hesitate to step forward and help. They want to, but they don't really understand what is needed.

I can't expect other people to know as much about my loved one's condition as I do. But I'd rather not have to explain over and over the nature of his condition and what he needs. Yet, if I don't give out information, how can I expect others to know how to help him? I know there are books, tapes, web sites, and organizations that offer information about his condition. Perhaps I could prepare a list of these resources for people who ask or need to know. Or I could loan them books and tapes I have found helpful. And I could ask my doctor or a support organization for informational literature to pass along. It might help to prepare a brief checklist of information specific to my loved one's situation and give that to people who want to help.

I seek help to teach others
about my loved one's needs.

Defenseless

I feel assaulted at times: I get discouraging news concerning my loved one's situation. People make harsh and thoughtless comments. I'm bombarded with information and decisions to make. With all these things coming at me, I feel defenseless. It's like getting hit by a truck.

This image of a truck coming at me can leave me feeling awfully small. What if I changed that image? I might feel bigger, less like a victim. I could play with that image of a truck in my mind or draw it on paper, picturing the truck as big as it feels and then shrinking it down to size. I could move it around or make it disappear. Suddenly it has less power. Using my imagination like this can alter my reality by altering my picture of it. So much of my fear and stress is the result of how I interpret or imagine things to be. Luckily, my imagination is unlimited and I can make changes.

*My creative imagination can free me
from any imagined doom.*

Blame and Humility

A lot of things go wrong when I'm taking care of my loved one. I tend to blame myself. I go over and over in my head what happened and how I could have handled it differently. I can become quite critical of myself and feel badly.

It is true, some things I've done have caused problems. I don't always like to admit that. It's humbling. But humility isn't all bad. Humility is simply being honest—acknowledging what has happened and making certain to neither exaggerate nor diminish my role in it. True humility helps me see each situation as realistically as possible. I don't make excuses for myself but I don't condemn myself either. I don't take on the blame for what others have done or for things I can't control, don't understand, or don't know. Once I'm clear about where the responsibility lies, I allow the situation to teach me rather than damage me.

I learn what I can from each problem that arises,
and take responsibility if I am at fault.

Attention to Details

As I comb my loved one's hair or tidy up a room, I find myself admiring what I do. These are little things, but when I give them my careful attention and do them well, I take pride in them. They make her life more pleasant and easier and that's important to me.

I know these routine tasks are taken for granted. But they are the activities that fill my day when I'm caring for her. They are what I accomplish and everyone likes to feel good about what they accomplish. I do feel good about these daily tasks, even if no one else notices. Of course I'm glad when someone says how nice my loved one or her room looks or when my loved one expresses appreciation, but mostly I feel a sense of satisfaction in simply doing things well. It does me good to stop once in a while and admire my handiwork.

My attention to detail is a source of pride.

Caring Enough To Rest

I'm determined to do everything I can to help my loved one. I give it my all, even though I know it would be good for me to get away sometimes. I think I should be able to manage everything myself if I just try hard enough. If I take a break to get some rest, people will think I don't care.

I do care a lot. And I want to give a lot to my loved one. But caring doesn't require that I be present one hundred percent of the time. It doesn't mean I must do everything myself. No one can reasonably expect that of me. Taking time for a break doesn't lessen my caring or commitment. Instead, I come back more refreshed and relaxed and better able to give care. And my situation seems more manageable. By getting rest, I am also caring for myself, which is my responsibility as well.

I take breaks to renew and refresh myself.

Decisions I Can't Control

I feel like a bystander at times. Other people are making decisions about what is best for my loved one and I have no say in the matter. If I offer an opinion, I fear being rebuffed. I feel powerless.

I am powerless over many things as a caregiver. It's best I admit that. It's wise for me to be clearly aware of when I have control and when I don't. When I don't, I step back and allow others to make their choice. Even though I may want a different result, the decision is not mine to make. I can state my preferences, and I am especially assertive if the decision will have a direct impact on me. But then I step back and turn my attention to matters over which I do have control. I ask my Spiritual Power for the strength and wisdom I need to stay detached.

> *I make the choices that are mine to make,*
> *and I allow others to make theirs.*

Community Support

I've always appreciated being part of a community, but I never knew how powerful community support could be until I became a caregiver. Friends, family, and strangers have all been there for us in ways I could never have imagined.

People care. In their busy lives, they make the time to be in touch, to help us out, to just sit and laugh and cry with us. We have received many gifts and free services. I have not always found it easy to accept all this generosity. I've always heard, "If you can't afford it, do without it." But I've had to break that rule to accept from others any number of things that I couldn't afford or that money could never pay for. I've been amazed how people have given things and then thanked me for the opportunity. I feel encircled in love.

Receiving the love of others is a way I can contribute to the circle of community.

Choices

I'm expected to be on hand to relieve my loved one's pain. When I can't be right there with her all the time, I feel guilty. Others resent my absence, too. I am "punished."

However, my presence is not always possible. I have other responsibilities that are also important to me. Of course, I would like to help more. But even if I were there, I can't guarantee I could relieve the pain or give enough help to satisfy everyone. I waver back and forth like this, thinking I should be there and then justifying why I'm not. There is no easy resolution. But it helps if I make a firm choice about how to schedule my day and then stick with it. Not that I can't reconsider the choice if situations change, but a continual rehashing of my decision is unhealthy. Let me just concern myself with carrying out my current choice and dismiss the other options for now.

Today I choose how and where I will help,
and I live with that choice.

Exercise

The work I do as a caregiver doesn't necessarily give me good exercise. I'm not getting enough aerobic, flexibility, and strengthening benefits. Yet I can't seem to find the time or the motivation to exercise right.

I know I feel better when I exercise, and I get things done with greater ease. Maybe that's where I need to start—by making a list of all the benefits I get from the right kind of exercise. With my list as a reminder, I can picture myself in a good mood, for example, and moving easily through my daily activities. Keeping my list handy will inspire me to stay faithful to an exercise plan. I would also be wise to plan a specific time in my daily schedule to exercise, just like I do with meals, so it becomes routine. I can start small, adding one activity a week. Once I start exercising and feel the benefits, I'll be glad I did it and I'll be able to give better care.

I'll do at least one exercise activity today
and make a plan for exercising tomorrow.

Family Patterns

Our family sometimes gets on each other's nerves. We argue over how to handle the care of our loved one. One person is always critical. Another wants to be in control. Another withdraws. The patterns are so familiar that we can usually predict what each other is going to say. The whole thing gets wearing.

I wonder what the family "rules" or values are that keep us repeating these patterns? Is it our family belief that no one can ever do enough? Is it that we're considered "good" only if we suffer? Does our family value saving money more than saving our sanity? It might help if I made a list of rules that we seem to live by. Maybe others in the family would help me create it. Then we could all be more aware of how we get tripped up by family rules and support each other in changing the patterns that keep us miserable.

I am willing to rethink the ways I behave with family members that do more harm than good.

Still Moments

I could use a stronger spiritual life. While I have my beliefs and religious practices, it's easy to forget them with the stresses of caregiving. But I haven't got time to sit and pray all day.

Still, I want my spiritual life to permeate every action in my life. One way to keep on track is to take advantage of still moments during the day. When I'm put on hold on the telephone, when I'm in line for a cashier or a freeway entrance, when commercials come on—anytime I'm asked to "wait" during the day is an opportunity for a still moment. It's my chance to focus inward, take a deep breath, dip into the still center of my being, and connect with my spiritual resources. I call to mind a brief prayer, an inspiring message, a line from a song, or a rejuvenating image, or simply absorb the stillness—anything that re-grounds me in my beliefs and reminds me that all is well.

I stop for still moments throughout my day.

Visitors

People are afraid to come visit. They don't like the smell, the looks, the sounds of sickness. For some, it brings back memories too sad for them. Others fear their own mortality. Still others just can't deal with pain. I want to invite people to come, but I'm afraid they won't.

Perhaps I could invite some people to visit just with me. I need company, too. It would even do me good to ask them to talk about things other than my loved one's condition. I could use a break from that. By letting them know I want a change of pace, that I'm not expecting them to give me a shoulder to cry on, I may make it easier for them to come. I can ask for that more personal kind of support from some people, of course, but others will be good company just by pleasantly distracting me from my daily preoccupation with caregiving.

I make visits easy and enjoyable.

Weather Report

Whatever the weather forecast, the real "weather" for the day centers around my loved one's condition. We get good news from the doctor or not such good news. A symptom lessens or worsens. A needed service becomes available or unavailable. We are constantly on guard, watching the changing conditions.

I can't change the weather and I can't change my loved one's condition. Nor can I change the many circumstances that affect us both. But I keep my internal weather "mostly fair and sunny" by staying close to my Spiritual Power. Even if there's a storm around me, I need never experience a power outage that leaves me in the dark and fearful. I have a backup source that keeps my lights on and helps me maintain a bright outlook.

Today is fair and sunny.

Trusting That I'll Have What I Need

What will happen if I run out of money? If I can't get the right kind of care arranged? If I run out of energy?

"What ifs" keep my mind spinning. They make me think that I'll never have enough or be enough, that disaster is just around the corner. I realize I'm slow to trust sometimes, but the truth is, things usually do work out in the end. Haven't I been surprised again and again by how an unexpected change in circumstances solved a problem? Haven't I come up with ideas that "kept the devil from my door?" Hasn't the goodness of others come through for me more than once?

I trust that I'll have what I need.

Feeling Selfish

I feel so selfish. I know my loved one needs a great deal of attention and support, but I don't always feel like giving it. I'm either too tired or I have other things I'd rather do. Then I feel guilty about feeling that way.

What a swirl of feelings! They'll keep me miserable and wear me out if I let them. I wonder where they come from. Do I expect myself to give one hundred percent all the time? Do I expect myself to give up all my other interests to give care to my loved one? Am I letting some "should" in my head dictate what I do, rather than looking at what's realistic and appropriate in this situation? Rather than judging myself harshly, I can evaluate what I'm doing with honesty and love, including self-love, and make any needed changes.

> *I am both loving and practical,*
> *and I am at peace with that.*

Catastrophes

An unpleasant incident can happen and then become so huge in my mind that I think it's a catastrophe. I devote my thoughts to it all day, or else I turn my attention completely to something else, trying to avoid escape thinking about it. Either way, it takes its toll.

I'm amazed at how often this happens. Something consumes my attention one day, and a few days later it's forgotten. I guess the good news is that most of the things that strike me as catastrophes aren't such a big deal in the end. Time passes and I get some perspective on them. The next time I get caught up in a mind swirl over a "catastrophe," it might help if I remember, this will pass. Tomorrow or next week, it will not seem that important. Like rain, it will end and something good may come of it.

This will pass.

Feeling Trapped

On a scale from one (feeling free) to ten (feeling trapped), too often I'm near ten. That's a danger zone for me, from which I'm likely to slide into resentment, discouragement, and anger—even hostility.

But my imagination can rescue me. I close my eyes and picture this "trapped" scale in my mind. I imagine where I am between one and ten at the current moment. Then, I imagine what it would be like to feel even more trapped than I do and what it would be like to feel less trapped. I ease myself up and down the scale and notice how my feelings change. Before long it becomes clear that "trapped" is only a thought I am having; and I can adjust my thoughts (and feelings) with a little help from my imagination. I have options, and with options comes freedom. I am always in charge of my thoughts, no matter what the outside circumstances.

I'm only as trapped as I think I am;
I can choose a new thought.

When Visitors Come

I've noticed that friends and family don't come around as much as they used to. Even when they do come, they sometimes say things that are hurtful or nosy. Or they stay too long and wear me out. I like having visitors, but sometimes it's more stressful than helpful.

I'm learning, though, to set limits with friends and family. When I get tired during their visit, I either excuse myself and go rest, or I invite them to come back at another time when I can be better company. I let them know how they can be helpful, and I avoid giving detailed answers to their questions if I find that doing so wears me out. When they say things I don't appreciate, I tell them directly how their words affect me and I ask them to stop. It takes self-respect and courage to set limits and be direct, but, once I do, I'm not a victim anymore. I'm in charge of my life—and my company.

I respect myself and insist that
others respect me as well.

Eating on the Run

I miss the pleasure of sitting down and leisurely eating a complete, healthy meal. With everyone tugging on my time and with my loved one's eating needs coming first, it's easy for me to skip meals or settle for quick high-carb, high-sugar snacks. Either I lose weight because I don't eat enough or put on weight because of the high-calorie snacking. Either way I end up hungry for real nourishment.

Just as my loved one needs to eat well, so do I. I need a healthy balance of satisfying foods each day. I also need to take the time to sit down and enjoy my food without rushing. And pleasant company can add tremendously to a meal's enjoyment. When I eat in a healthy and peaceful way, I feel better. I am "filled up." I don't have to keep stuffing myself with junk, and my body and mind are better equipped to provide the care that is demanded of me.

I will sit down to at least one balanced meal today and arrange to eat with someone I enjoy very soon.

Replenishing Activities

My responsibilities wear me out. There's not only the caregiving, but the cooking, shopping, repairs, family demands, and meetings to go to. It seems like there's no end. As busy as I am, when I finally get a few minutes for myself, it's so easy to flop down in front of the TV. I can just stare at it until I get my mind off of things or fall asleep. But I have to admit I don't get much out of it. It's more like a pacifier.

I know I can choose other activities that will replenish me rather than just numb my mind. I can put on a meditation tape to help me relax and center myself. I can do a few minutes of yoga. I can read something inspiring or stimulating. I can give my arms, legs, or feet a gentle massage. I can do some stretching exercises. When I do little things for myself that I enjoy, I feel so much better. The TV is a poor substitute for genuine self-care.

I will make a list of self-replenishing activities and do something on the list each day.

My Body Aches

My body seems to hurt everywhere. I'm on my feet for what seems like hours. I'm constantly lifting and bending and pushing. I know I should let up, but how can I, with all I have to do?

My body won't hold up for long if I don't give it some relief. I can stop briefly and rest between activities, even if only for a few seconds. I can do some strengthening or flexibility exercises to keep me in shape. A massage or vinegar bath could ease my muscle strain. Perhaps I can even learn some ways of doing tasks that take less effort and create less strain. There are classes and videotape programs that teach such things. I could check with my doctor to learn more or ask friends or a librarian about resources. With new ways of doing things and a little positive attention, my body might feel a lot better. If the work is still too much for me, it may be time to turn the physical care over to someone else.

My body is my friend and I will treat it well.

Surrender

A lot of spiritual books say I should "surrender" to God. But I don't like the idea of surrendering at all. I've got to hold on. I can see what needs to be done and I'm determined to make it happen.

But I get tired and tense trying to work everything out, and some things really are beyond my control. Maybe it doesn't make sense to keep trying so hard to do something that isn't working. Yet it's hard to think of giving up. Perhaps I don't have to give up. I could try opening up instead. It's possible my perspective has gotten a little narrow with all the pressure I've been under as a caregiver. I could let up a little, consider what others have to say, and open up to the greater wisdom of my Spiritual Power. Surrendering may not limit me. It could give me more to work with.

I open up and surrender to a greater good.

Awkward Feelings

Even though I have a close relationship with the person I'm caring for, I don't feel loving toward her every single minute. Sometimes she annoys me; occasionally I despise her. When others are around at such times, I don't want to show a phony affection for her, but I don't want them to think I am uncaring either.

Every relationship has its uncomfortable times. And though it's not appropriate to talk about these things with every visitor, some people genuinely appreciate when I'm authentic with them about the ebb and flow of my feelings. Of course, I avoid being critical of my loved one and just talk about what's going on with me. It helps to tell others how I feel, especially people I trust, people who won't judge me. By being real, I get a sense of relief.

> *I accept the changes in my feelings*
> *and I expect others to do the same.*

Blame

I get blamed for how my loved one is doing. People think that if I were doing something more or getting different help or using their favorite remedy, he would be better. Whenever I make a decision about his care, someone questions it. Family members can get downright nasty about it. I'm tired of taking the blame.

Since I'm the one who makes the decisions, I'm the one to take the flack. But other people are not in my shoes. I'm the one who has to sort through all the information and weigh the choices. Maybe there are better options for my loved one. I choose what to do based on what I know. I can do no better than that. I'm just as disappointed as others when he isn't doing as well as he might. But I can't control everything about his condition. I can only make the choices that seem best to me. That's good enough. Other people can cast blame, but I don't have to accept it.

I make the best choices I can, and that's good enough.

Finding Meaning

I wonder why I've ended up as a caregiver. It seems so strange. This is not what I had planned for my life. It has demanded far more of me than I ever imagined I could endure. Why is this happening?

I know there are no easy answers to this question, but it's important for me to find some meaning in this experience. Otherwise I'll go crazy. Maybe there's no specific "reason" for this happening at all. Maybe its meaning is what I decide it to be. I can view this caregiving experience as my calling, at least for this part of my life. I've been asked to do it, and I've chosen to say yes. I am where I belong for now. The experience is changing me. I am finding new strengths and uncovering weaknesses. I am learning who I can count on. I am gaining a clearer sense of what matters to me.

My life has more meaning because I am a caregiver,
and I'm grateful for that.

Loss of Favorite Pastimes

My loved one and I used to go places together, play games, create good times with each other. Now so many of those activities are lost to us. We have a hard time finding much we can enjoy doing together.

It's true we can't do many of the old fun activities, at least not in the same way. But we can still find small ways to keep alive the fun we used to have. Putting on old music reminds us of our favorite places and tends to wake up the memory in our bodies. We can still move a little bit like we used to. We may not be able to play our favorite games as well as we once did, but looking at photos of us in action can bring a few grins. Even pretending to shuffle a deck of cards or swing a racket or bat, combined with a wink and a few sound effects, gets us laughing. A few shared moments of enjoyment reconnect us and help us forget our troubles.

I can adapt favorite pastimes to create pleasant reunions with my loved one.

No Expectations

When I stop to look in on my loved one, and she is worse again, it's easy to get thrown into feeling hopeless. After seeing progress and getting my hopes up, the bad news hits and my expectations crumble for the umpteenth time.

This cycle of progress followed by new problems can wear on my spirit. Sometimes it seems as if it would be easier to stop hoping, even to stop caring. Hopeful expectations are too big an investment to have dashed again and again. I wonder if it's possible to keep on caring deeply and giving all I can to help my loved one without getting caught up in expectations. Could I just be a caring observer? Could I watch and wait with no hope? Could I trust that whatever happens is the right thing to happen? A scary thought. Yet, I can do that if I rely on my Spiritual Power. Then, I don't need a certain turn of events to find peace of mind.

I surrender to what each moment brings.

Patience with Other Caregivers

Some people get so irritated with my loved one. They don't understand how hard it is for him. They expect too much. They want him to be compliant and grateful all the time, and that's impossible. It hurts me to watch him being treated this way.

I'm sure that everyone involved in giving him care feels the effects of the ongoing demands. It isn't easy, and he isn't always cooperative or even pleasant. I want to be compassionate, not critical, toward all those involved. When I can step in and offer some relief or lend an understanding ear, I do. That can help someone get a needed break and regain some patience. If need be, I directly confront someone who is being too cross or demanding. I know I can't control anyone else's behavior, but I do what I can to make life as pleasant as possible for my loved one and to be patient with everyone involved.

I show compassion for other caregivers
and do what I can to soften their impatience.

Self-deprivation

I sometimes feel guilty enjoying myself when my loved one is suffering so much. If I go out for a nice meal or buy new clothes or do some other normally pleasant activity, I feel I have to keep it a secret. Or I think I have to make up for it by depriving myself of something so she won't have to feel jealous.

In reality, nothing I do to deprive myself improves her life. Rather, if I am enjoying my life, I am a happier person. I'm more pleasant to be around and more likely to bring fresh energy to my caregiving role. If she becomes jealous, that's not my responsibility. Of course I don't want to flaunt my activities in front of her. That would be cruel. But I don't have to hide them either. They are part of who I am. I am compassionate and understanding in talking with her about any jealousy or resentment she may feel. If, however, she tries to make me feel guilty, I can reject her manipulation.

I have a right to happiness.

Tension Busters

Certain things are set in my life right now. I can't change them. I don't like them and I wish they'd go away; but they're here to stay, at least for a while. I could get mighty angry about them, but that wouldn't do much good.

I do feel angry some of the time though. I have to admit it. But I've also found some ways to work off my anger. I play golf or softball, or I clean house or dig in the garden. In getting physically active, I get lost in what I'm doing and I get a good work-out. It doesn't change things but it takes my mind off my miseries, I have some fun, and I see some results. I always come back feeling like I can make it for a few more days.

I regularly absorb myself in activities that energize and refresh me.

Saying and Singing Affirmations

When I get overtired or discouraged in my efforts to care for my loved one, I tend to say a lot of negative things to myself: I can't manage. I don't know how to do this. It's all my fault. My running stream of negative thoughts gets me down.

But when I remember to say affirmations, I quickly turn my thinking around. I keep handy a written list of these positive statements, declaring what I know to be true when I'm in my best state of mind: I am highly capable. I learn easily when I am patient with myself. I'm doing the best I can and that's good enough. These affirmative statements strengthen my resolve and remind me of the highest truth about myself. I feel better when I say them. I find them especially helpful when I put them to music. Singing them opens my throat and my heart, generating more energy, power, and love.

I sing the truth to lift me to freedom.

The Unknown

The hardest part of dealing with my loved one's condition can be not knowing what is going on. All the uncertainty about the diagnosis and prognosis, about whether treatments will work, about the availability of particular services—it's agonizing. I want answers!

Yet, I know I can't always have them right away. In some cases, I never get them. Uncertainty is a given in life. It helps when I accept that. I can choose to view the uncertainties I experience as a witness, without expectation. I simply observe the comings and goings of what is happening, placing no demands on any of it. I set aside what could be or might be and attend to what is. Nothing is more mysterious. Nothing is more sacred. Rather than run from ambiguity, or try to change it, I plunge myself into it and discover its secrets. I surrender to my Spiritual Power present at its center and allow that to carry me through.

I am open to the gifts that lie within the unknown.

What's Normal

When my loved one appears "normal," I tend to expect him to behave normally. So do other people. I can be taken aback when suddenly he does something disruptive or offensive that he can't help.

Caregiving requires watchfulness. It's up to me to remember the limitations my loved one is dealing with, even when they're not obvious to others. If he does things that are inappropriate, I ask myself whether his action could be the result of his condition. If so, I treat it as I would a physical problem. I help him out, or I clean up the mess if need be. His action could, of course, have nothing to do with his condition and be the result of a choice he has full control over. In that case, I respond as I would to someone with normal capabilities and expect him to take responsibility. It is a fine line. I can't always expect myself to know how to call it. I am gentle with myself, and with him, as we make our way through these dilemmas together.

I stay alert and loving, ready to forgive quickly.

Bitterness

I get bitter sometimes. I wonder why all this had to happen. I resent my life being so unsettled by the problems my loved one is having. I lose appreciation for much of anything. I feel grim.

It helps if I can choose something to smile about, just one thing. Even if I have to start by pretending there is something I appreciate. If I'm tired enough of my bitterness, it seems worth it to come up with something positive in my life that I can focus on for a little while. Then I can look for one more thing—and one more—and before long, my lips are curling up from a deep frown to only a mild frown. After a while, a smile becomes a possibility. I don't push it. I just ease myself gently out of my grim hole into a bit of daylight.

I am willing to look for something
I can appreciate today—and risk smiling.

Toughening Up?

I'm used to doing things for myself. I don't like to ask for help. I don't want to bother other people. They'll think I should just toughen up and handle things. But I don't know if I can manage everything alone.

I'm glad I have an independent spirit. It has given me the strength to do a lot of things. But I'm not a superhero. No one expects me to do the impossible, and neither should I. Maybe, instead of toughening up, I could soften up a little and ask for help. I'll feel more like I'm part of the community and I won't be so alone. I have limits and if I fall apart from trying to do too much, I won't be much good for my loved one or myself. It helps to remember that I wasn't put on this earth alone. I'm glad to help others when they need it, and I'm sure other people feel the same way about helping me. That's what it means to be part of a community—people both giving and accepting care.

I seek support to keep up my strength.

Someone to Talk To

I have done things and thought things I'm ashamed of as a caregiver. Sometimes I have a hard time admitting them, let alone forgiving myself. I have a barrelful of feelings: resentment, fear, jealousy, sorrow. My mind gets in a spin about all these things and they weigh on me. I feel alone and confused.

When I'm experiencing such a swirl of disturbing thoughts and feelings, I know it helps to write them down on paper. That way I can get a clearer picture of how I'm coping with what's going on. Then it helps to find someone I trust to hear me out—a member of the clergy, a good friend, a counselor. It's time I tell someone what is deeply troubling me. In revealing my secrets, I free myself from them. I find acceptance and forgiveness. I no longer feel so alone.

I am willing to reveal myself to a loving and accepting listener so I can find peace.

Should I Tolerate the Mess?

I'm not sure what to do when my loved one's living area is constantly messy. I don't like to see the way things are being neglected. I'd offer to help, but it might seem like I'm butting in where I don't belong. And some things I can't do anything about.

This looks like one of those "Serenity Prayer" situations. Would I do best to just accept how things are and keep my attention focused on giving heartfelt care to my loved one? Or is there a way I could help change the situation? Are my standards too high or is this a genuinely unsafe or unsanitary situation? Does this call for courage to take a risk and speak up? Should I just step in and start cleaning? Is there someone else I can ask for assistance? If I'm not quite sure, I can "shhhh" my tumbling thoughts, ask my Spiritual Power for guidance, and trust what comes to me.

I will ask for guidance and act on it today.

Pity

When I see my loved one struggling with basic everyday activities, I feel so sorry for him. I know how hard it is for him to cope with these limitations, and I so wish he could be normal. I do everything I can to make things easier, but I can't fix what's wrong. My heart breaks when I watch him.

I know it's up to him to find his own way of coping with his limitations. My pity won't help him. What will be helpful is to keep remembering that he is capable of handling what he must face. In fact, I've been inspired at times by how resilient and courageous he has been. Knowing that he has a Spiritual Power to help him, I can trust that he will be all right even if he has hard things to face. I will be there to support him all the way and to relish his victories.

I see my loved one as capable and growing.

Repaying People

I marvel at the care my loved one receives. Professionals, volunteers, family members, and friends have all been wonderful. They've shown such unselfish devotion, I don't know how I can adequately thank them.

I feel blessed by all that people have done. I feel like I owe a big debt. But I know I cannot possibly repay it. And that's all right. People are giving because they want to give. They are doing what is important for them to do. They are getting rewards in their own way. It is not my job to repay but to receive. I say thank you in small ways, and that is enough. If I keep worrying about how to repay people, I may miss the opportunity to simply accept and enjoy what is being given. The best way to repay someone is to be a gracious receiver.

I gratefully receive the kindness of others.

Resentment

At times I get mighty angry at some of my family and friends. They say the most thoughtless things; they don't show up when they're needed; they interfere with what I'm trying to do. I resent being the one who's expected to handle everything and then clean up their mistakes of top of it.

But this resentment becomes a cancer eating away my happiness. I spend too much time worrying about what they're doing or not doing. I don't want to give their actions so much attention and power. I'm going to practice detaching myself from what they say and do. I'll take what actions I can to gain their cooperation, but when they make a mess of things, I'll let them clean up after themselves. I'll ask my Spiritual Power, my friends, or my support group to help me keep my attention on my own actions, not on what others do. I refuse to let resentment destroy my spirit.

*I free myself from the cancer of resentment
and do what is mine to do.*

Privacy

It helps to talk to someone else about all that my loved one and I are dealing with. But of course I want to respect my loved one's privacy, so I'm not sure how much I should reveal.

I need someone trustworthy to confide in. But even with this person, I take care in what personal details I reveal about my loved one. She has the right to decide what she wants others to know about her situation and her reactions to it. It is her life, her body, her story. So, before I discuss information about her to a confidante, it's important to ask her about what she is comfortable having people know. Of course, I can freely reveal my own experiences, including my reaction to what is happening to her. When I keep the focus on my own activities, I am speaking most authentically and I am more likely to receive the kind of understanding and support I want.

I speak the deepest truths when I stay focused on my own reality.

Separate Feelings

When my loved one is down in the dumps, I have trouble keeping my spirits up. I try not to get dragged down, but after a while his bad moods get to me.

I want to do everything I can to remain upbeat and optimistic, but it's unrealistic to think I can maintain a positive outlook all the time. I will feel down sometimes. But I don't want to take on anyone else's moods. When my loved one is having a hard time, I can acknowledge that and show compassion, but it will not help anyone if I take on his feelings myself. One good way to keep myself clearly separate from his feeling is to pay close attention to my own. Am I sad, fearful, angry? Am I irritated, confused, excited? Am I eager, concerned, delighted? Am I surly, edgy, curious?

I will name and claim one feeling I'm having today that is different from my loved one's feelings.

Satisfying Moments

When I make a decision that turns out well for my loved one, or when I am able to soothe her with physical support or a word of comfort, it's gratifying. I feel satisfied, even proud, that I've been able to help her.

It surprises me that I get so many gifts while I'm giving care to someone else. I didn't expect to get the extra bursts of adrenaline that come from being of service. I especially enjoy the pleasure of accomplishing things that seem difficult. If it provides any relief for my loved one, I feel good about my effort. When I see positive results, I get even more energy. Not everything I do works out as I hoped, of course. But when I feel a little discouraged, it helps to recall the satisfying moments and draw energy from them once again.

I take time today to feel satisfaction
in what I'm able to give.

Soul Work

I do more than just take care of my loved one. At times, I am her voice, her advocate, and even her mind. When she is unable to think clearly or speak for herself, I become the conduit for the work of her soul. I listen attentively on her behalf and allow her soul's guide to make clear to me what she needs.

This task is calling me to a higher level of consciousness. Not only am I acting for myself now, but for her highest good. I listen for her guidance as well as my own. More is available to me than when I have only myself to consider. In my loved one's suffering state, her Spiritual Power is at work and I am taken into partnership to help carry out that work. I feel myself raised up, given direction, given peace. I have been invited to become the instrument, and I am willing. I know that what I do for my loved one is preparing me for the soul work of my own that is to come.

I attend reverently to the soul work of my loved one as well as my own.

The Best and the Worst

I've seen the worst come out in both my loved one and me since he has developed health problems. We have had our moments of being nasty, selfish, stubborn, indifferent—even mean.

But oddly enough, I've also seen the best in us come out. Not that we've agreed on everything. We've clashed plenty. But we've also found times when our care for one another surmounted all the chaos and crises and uncertainty brought on by the health problems. Like war buddies, we got closer because we had to. No one else had been through what we were going through together. We were the only ones who understood what was at stake and what price had to be paid. We rose above the staggering details to remember how much we meant to each other. Memories of these intimate "best" moments sustain me whenever the "worst" behaviors slip through.

Profound mutual respect keeps us at our best.

New Possibilities

Some of the problems that have come up for me and my loved one seem insurmountable. I can't see a way out. I feel disheartened.

If I think back, I've been here before; I've been in situations that seemed hopeless. And then something would change. Something would happen that I could never have anticipated, and I would get a break. Where I had fretted and worried and given up, I now had new possibilities. It was almost like a miracle. Remembering those experiences keeps me from giving in to discouragement. My trust is renewed. There is almost certainly something unexpected awaiting me if I'm open to it.

I'm open to new possibilities.

When Day Is Done

At the end of my day, I tend to fret about what I didn't get done and what I did wrong. I worry about what people are going to think about some of the things I did. On and on I review the day and then I can't wind down, can't get to sleep.

When the day is done, it's time for me to rest. But first I have to put the day's happenings to rest. I'm done. They're done. The day is over. Rather than agonize over the day and criticize myself, I can turn my attention to what went well. There is always much to appreciate from the day if I take notice. I can also forgive myself and others for any failings that showed up. And I can make plans to set right what went wrong. If there is still some unfinished business from the day that I can't quite figure out how to resolve, I can surrender it in prayer, trusting the outcome to One who is wiser than me.

I let today be finished at day's end.

Time to Speak Up

When my loved one's condition deteriorates, those of us close to him need to make plans about increased levels of care, maybe even move him to a new place, and decide how to dispose of his belongings. But how can I bring up the subject without seeming like I'm delivering bad news?

They say the truth is supposed to set you free. I wish I could believe that. I can see what needs to be done, but others might be afraid to face it. Actually, I'm afraid, too. Maybe that's the real truth I should bring up if I want to start a conversation about the changes we are all facing. I could admit that I'm afraid and unsure what to do and ask the others for help in looking for solutions. My openness might encourage theirs. But if they're too afraid to respond right away, I don't press the issue. I allow them the time they need to face their fears in their own way.

I am patient with myself and those close to me
as we face the fear of change and loss.

Who's in Charge?

From day to day, my role seems to change. Some days all the decisions are mine to make. Other days my loved one is capable of handling choices. Many times her professional helpers are in charge. I have to step forward and then step back again. It gets confusing.

Because there are few "rules" to govern this situation, I have to stay attentive. I want to be aware when others are in a better position to know what is needed than me. I honor my loved one's abilities and preferences as much as possible, yet I need to take charge when he's faltering. I respect the competence of the professional caregivers and the regulations that guide their work, but I also make sure that my loved one's needs and preferences are respected. There is a kind of reverence for the rhythm of these relationships that I work to maintain.

I take charge as needed, while respecting the roles of everyone involved.

Spiritual Beliefs

As I watch my loved one struggling, I realize that he doesn't have the same beliefs and values I do. I feel sure that mine would help him. I try to talk to him about them but he is not always receptive.

I realize I cannot give my spiritual values to him. What's most important is that I live by them myself. By practicing love and respect and patience, I am giving him the benefits of my beliefs. I also want to be alert and responsive to whatever spiritual spark I see in him. It may not show up in the same way it does for me, but I can trust that the universal Spiritual Power has the capacity to transform the ways of humans into higher ways. I let go of any fears I have for my loved one and settle into love and trust. I remember I am not in charge of his spiritual destiny and I surrender control.

I honor the life of the spirit,
however it shows up in my loved one.

Independence

Sometimes other people offer to help and I push the help away, saying, "That's okay. I can manage." Then, before long, I find myself thinking, "This is too hard for me. Can't my friends and family understand that I need help?"

I wonder if my loved one does the same thing, refusing help at times out of habit or concern for me, and then becoming resentful that I don't do more for him. It's tricky knowing when to be independent and when to be interdependent. I guess we've been trying to figure out the right balance since we were kids. It's easy to err on the side of being way too independent. Yet there is something admirable and satisfying in the determination to do things for yourself. I want to respect that inborn desire for independence in both of us. At the same time, I want to be aware when turning to others for help is in our best interest.

I value my independence,
but I'm smart enough to know when I need help.

Strengths

I've had to learn some new skills as a caregiver and take on some tasks I'm not especially good at. I feel incompetent. I want to give the best care possible, but I fail to get things done right all too often. I get very frustrated with myself.

When I focus on my incompetence and my weaknesses, my self-worth takes a dip. I can quickly sink into a black hole of self-criticism and discouragement. That helps no one. Although I'm not good at everything, I certainly contribute a lot of skills and strengths to the care of my loved one. I tend to take them for granted and forget I have them. I could start making a list of the assets I bring to caregiving. For the list to be complete, I might have to stop and think about positive comments others have made about my strengths. That might be worth doing, just to put my efforts in perspective and help me maintain a healthy self-esteem.

I focus on my strengths and keep building on them.

Over-Responsibility

I try hard to do all I can for my loved one, but it never seems enough. I think of all the things I could be doing to make her life better if I only tried a little harder. Guilt is a constant companion.

Then, every once in a while my loved one will say something to me like, "You're so nice to me" and I just melt. I feel comforted. At the same time, I feel sad. I recognize how difficult it is for her to be in a situation where she has to depend on me continually for help. I'm sad her life is so hard. But when she reminds me in a special way that I am a comfort to her and that I do a lot for her, it eases my guilt. I realize I may have been expecting too much of myself. Yes, I want to help her all I can, but some of her problems I can't take away no matter how hard I try. And I don't need to carry around guilt for them.

I give what I can to my loved one and that is enough.

Rage as Energy

Any number of things can set me off: something my loved one does, a helper's incompetence, my own mistakes. I get so furious I explode. When rage takes hold of me, I can end up doing hurtful things and then feeling badly afterwards.

If I'm honest with myself, I have to admit that rage doesn't really take hold of me. It's a surge of energy all right, but I control the switch. If I watch myself when I get set to explode, I can see exactly when I make the decision to let loose. That's the moment when I could turn this energy surge into productive or creative uses. Instead of releasing it destructively, I could use it to dig up a garden, scrub a floor, or blow up balloons. Or if I want to give my fury free rein, I could step into the bathroom, close the door, and stomp my feet to let off steam without hurting anyone. Then I'll be through with my rage, and I will have energy to move on.

A feeling of rage reveals a source of energy
I can draw on.

Silent Presence

When my loved one is suffering through especially difficult times, I feel so helpless. I try to find ways to ease the agony, but sometimes there is nothing that can be done.

At times like these, I just sit with her and hold her hand. I know it must be terrifying for her to go through this, and I don't want her to be alone. I don't have to say anything, just being with her is enough. I know my presence gives her strength and reassurance, and somehow being with her is a comfort to me as well. I resist the temptation to busy myself just so I can feel like I'm doing something. What she needs is my quiet, attentive presence. When I give her that, I get to know her experience more deeply and that is a gift to me.

I am a still and silent companion in the hard times.

Receiving Care

I never thought it would turn out like this, me being a caregiver. The truth is, I don't much feel like doing it. It doesn't seem fair that I had to give up my own plans to take care of my loved one. I know it might seem selfish of me, but at times I wish I had someone to take care of me.

Of course, I do have a Caregiver. I'm not in this alone. But I wish I felt that reassuring Presence more than I do. I guess the first thing I need to do is allow myself to be cared for. I'm willing to do that now. I'm going to take a deep breath, let go, and trust that a Power greater than myself has open arms waiting for me to surrender all my troubles. I'm going to let in the ever-present, tender love and know that all is well.

Today I will remember that I am cared for
and let the love in.

Support from Other Caregivers

I know there are others like me—caregivers who face what I face, feel what I feel. It would be nice to talk to someone who's going through a similar experience. I would like to get some ideas about how other people manage, not just the physical matters, but the disturbing thoughts and the feelings that get so huge.

I could look for a caregiver support group. Some religious organizations, community centers, and health care organizations have them. Or I could start one myself. I could ask around and see if there are a couple of people who would get together with me at regular times. Maybe some of the professional caregivers that help my loved one could suggest some names. We could read and discuss a meditation or choose a topic of our own or check in on how each person is doing. Mostly what I want is a group in which we listen to each other with genuine understanding. We all need to be understood.

I join with other caregivers for mutual support.

Making the Most of Today

I get so caught up in the things I have to do some days that I feel like I'm just going through the motions. I move from one thing to the next and hardly stop to take a rest. When the day is done, I don't know where it went.

But each day is a gift. I want to savor all its richness. Especially when I spend time with my loved one, I want to make the most of it. I want to listen carefully, speak thoughtfully, and catch every glimpse of beauty I can. Every day I want to make sure I laugh and sing at least twice. I want to smell something spicy. I want to watch for the surprises and also create a few. I want to pray and celebrate and taste glory. And I want to take time to rest and let it all sink in.

I am awake to the gift that this day offers and I intend to make the most of it.

Manipulation

My loved one issues threats. Sometimes they're subtle. She implies that something awful will happen to her if I don't do what she wants. She's just trying to manipulate me and I resent it.

I'm often tempted to give in. I think that will keep her safe. What I'm actually doing is supporting her manipulative behavior and giving her license to repeat it. But I'm afraid to call her on it. What if something bad does happen to her? I'd never forgive myself. However, that guilt-ridden kind of thinking is what keeps me stuck in this mire of manipulation. I have a right to say no to her requests. I'm not responsible for how she responds, nor for any disasters that might happen. As hard as it might seem to stay detached from her demands and keep my own authority, it is healthier for both of us if I do. If need be, I can seek professional guidance to assist me.

I live by my own authority and I allow others theirs.

Lonely Times

I'm alone more than I would like to be. I don't understand why people don't come around or call more than they do. But I suppose they just don't want to be bothered with people who have problems.

The long hours—even days—spent caring for my loved one alone can become depressing. I wonder what I could do to be more connected with others. Who could I invite over? What attitude would be most helpful when I ask them? Do I consider myself worthy of their company? Do I have some resentments or judgments about them that are getting in my way and in theirs? Are my fears stopping me? Do I let one person's "no" discourage me? Is my pride standing in the way of honestly letting others know how lonely and discouraged I am? It might help to consider ways I could soften any resistance I feel about letting people into my life. I do this gently, recognizing my own vulnerability since undertaking the care of my loved one.

I let others know they are wanted and welcome.

Tough News

Some days I just can't believe that "everything is going to turn out all right." Nothing is turning out all right. One piece of misery piles up on another. I start to lose faith.

I want to keep my spirits up, to believe in the best outcome. Yet some days I don't feel I have the strength to do it. Shocking news comes in multiples and takes a toll. I feel traumatized and want to retreat. These are the days I look for a quiet place to recoup. I don't push myself to believe anything. I just nurse my wounds and recover. I write in my journal or have a talk with a close friend. Or I am still: I lie on a beach or rock myself or soak in the tub. My spirit needs a rest. I let the anguish I feel register in my bones and I mourn the loss of hope. In time I may find my way back to believing, but I make no promises.

I give myself time to recover from tough news.

Living in Today

I spend a lot of my time wondering and worrying about what will happen tomorrow, next week, next year. I get fearful that my loved one won't be able to manage, and neither will I. I'm afraid that money, time, and energy will run out.

It's easy to get hooked into concentrating on the future. And of course it's wise to prepare for the future as best I can. But keeping my thoughts churning about possible future catastrophes is a waste of time and energy. It raises my blood pressure and makes me tense and unhappy. If I spend my energy absorbed in tomorrow's potential problems, I can't enjoy whatever is in front of me right now. The present moment is really all I have, and I don't want to miss it.

I leave the future to the future and live in the now.

My Own Feelings

I can tell in a minute when my loved one's feelings change. Whether he's upset or scared or down in the dumps, I'm right there with him. I get so caught up in his moods sometimes that I almost feel his feelings more than he does. I don't know where he stops and I start.

Our love has brought us close together, but we are still separate people. If I over-identify with his feelings, I'm invading his domain and in danger of losing myself. His feelings are important, but so are mine. I can observe and appreciate what he is going through, but his experience is unique to him and he has his own story, his own emotional life, to live out. By immersing myself in his emotions, I'm not paying due attention to my own story and a part of me dies. I may benefit from writing down my own feelings when I'm away from him to gain practice in knowing what they are.

My feelings are my own and I value them.

Lighten Up

Everything feels so heavy sometimes. I get worn out and discouraged. Every little thing that happens feels like such a big deal.

But I suspect that I've made some things into a much bigger deal than they are. I waste energy fretting over these small things and have little left for matters of real concern. It helps if I widen my perspective. Within the whole history of my life, any one incident represents only a moment of time. It will pass. In the long run, it will probably seem like no big deal. Perhaps I could experiment with taking that view toward some of my current problems. No big deal! I could lighten up, brush them off, crack a smile, and see what happens. The problems might seem smaller and I might feel better. In that case, I'd have more energy to focus on matters of greater importance.

I can lighten up and say, "No big deal!"

Resistance to Talking about Feelings

My loved one wants me to sit down and talk with her about feelings, but I've got too much to do. I wish I could do a better job of attending to her emotional needs, but it's all I can do to get the chores done and errands run.

Managing the practical things is what I'm good at, so that's what I do. It wears me out, but I do it gladly so that my loved one is well taken care of. I'm not as good at talking about feelings, though. I think I'm afraid it will be too much for me to listen to her say how hard this situation is for her. I'm afraid to admit how hard it is for me. I figure if I just keep busy, I'll get through this. But I know I'm missing something when I don't take a little time now and then to just sit with her and give her my undivided attention. Her heart, as well as her body, needs my care. My heart needs to make the connection, too.

Making a heart connection with my loved one is a priority on my to-do list today.

Acknowledging Others

Everyone in the family is affected by the condition my loved one is struggling with. We all have a hard time with what's she's going through and how it has changed our lives as well, yet we tend to expect a lot from each other. I wonder if we could find a way to lighten the load for all of us.

We are giving so much because we want to. But even when people give unselfishly, it feels good to be acknowledged and appreciated. That's one small thing I could do for my family. I could tell them "Good job" or "Nice going" when I appreciate something they have done. It might brighten their day. A written note acknowledging their contributions is another nice touch. If I want some acknowledgement myself, I can remind others that I too could use a boost now and then. If they come through, it's important not to dismiss their kindness by saying something like, "It was nothing." I simply say, "Thanks."

I welcome appreciation and I give it freely.

Feeling Out of Control

I must be nuts. That's how I feel some days. Everything seems out of control. I want to do what's right for my loved one, but nothing is working out, no matter how hard I try. Things are falling apart. I don't know what to do.

In this state of mind, I'm being driven at high speed by my irrational thoughts. It helps to take my foot off the gas long enough to adjust my thinking. Then I can see it's a little grandiose to think that I am responsible for everything turning out all right. It's time to take the pressure off myself and remember that the outcome is in the hands of Someone greater than me. The answers I need for the present dilemmas are at hand. But I'll have to be willing to loosen my grip on the steering wheel before I can recognize them and take hold of them.

*Today I'll make a list of what I can't control
and turn it over to my Spiritual Power.*

Beyond My Limits

There are moments when my loved one's condition brings me to my knees. Frozen with grief or terror or fury, I can't function. Everything I thought I knew, or thought I was capable of, seems to vanish. I feel alone and lost.

At times like this, I can't bury my feelings any longer. I don't have the strength to hold back whatever I've been too afraid to admit. I fall into the arms of whoever is nearby and rage or shake or sob uncontrollably. I am in my most vulnerable state, but they can't truly comfort me. This is a time to become nakedly honest with myself. I can no longer pretend I have the strength or moral superiority I don't have. Hope vanishes. When all my walls have come down and I have nowhere to hide, all that's left to turn to is my Spiritual Power. I eventually become still, peaceful, with no more need to run or hide or fear.

When pushed to the limits,
I surrender to the Limitless.

Caught up in My Role

I get very wrapped up in my role as a helper sometimes. I take the ups and downs of my loved one personally, as if I alone am responsible. I start to measure my worth by whether I did "a good job" or not.

But my role as helper is just that. It's something I do for my loved one, but it's not me. It is an activity, and if I step back a little to observe, I can watch myself doing my helping activities and then doing other things. Though very important, my caregiving role is not my whole identity. It's part of what I do, and I'm not the only one who can do it. My worth does not depend on what I do for my loved one nor how good a job I do. My value is in my being, not my doing, not my role as helper. In remembering that, I am freer.

I am more than the care I give.

Clueless

I've read a lot about my loved one's condition. I've consulted experts. I've studied the symptoms and treatments. Still, much of the time I don't know the right thing to do. I feel clueless.

"I don't know" has been so hard to admit. I used to think that if I just got enough information or tried hard enough, I'd find the answers. As a caregiver, it's my job to know. I often imagine that someone else in my situation would be doing a much better job, knowing exactly what would work. But, of course, no one has a perfect prescription for my loved one's situation. So the best answer at any given moment is whatever I decide, based on what I've learned and my best judgment. I continue to seek additional guidance from others, but ultimately, my inner guidance is the final judge. That is all I need to know.

> *What I know at this moment*
> *is enough for this moment.*

Costume Play

Not every day has to be a serious one. I want to keep my spirits high and help my loved one do the same. We ought to be able to have some fun, even if we can't go out and have a good time the way we used to.

I wonder what would happen if I got playful and put on a costume. Anything would work—a goofy hat, a blanket draped over me, a makeshift mask, someone else's shoes. I could become anyone I choose and be as silly or dramatic as I want. It could give me a whole different perspective on my day. I could bring my loved one in on the act, and anyone else I could recruit. It would definitely take the edge off things and laughter is almost a sure thing. What have I got to lose … except a frown?

I can trade my everyday costume
for a more playful one.

Complaints and Accusations

My loved one doesn't always appreciate all I do for him. He complains, he tries to manipulate me into doing more, he accuses me of being selfish, of neglecting or mistreating him. It's hard enough for me to do all I do without having to take grief from him on top of it.

Sometimes I want to scream at him for being so ungrateful and for adding to my burden with his attitude. Other times I try to be understanding, knowing he's not himself in his condition. In either case, I can't make him change his attitude. What I can do is simply reject his unjust complaints, and accusations. Since they don't fit me, I don't have to accept them. No need to waste any effort defending myself. Instead, I gather my energy, reassure myself that I'm doing the best I can, and I tell him I won't accept his negative judgments about me.

*I know the truth about myself,
and no one else's opinion can change that.*

Keeping Friendships

Friends don't call or come around as much as they used to. I can't do things with them as often, and they probably get tired of hearing me talk about the ups and downs of caregiving. I understand, but I also miss them, and I get angry that they have pulled away.

I know my friends care. They rallied around me at first. Perhaps they don't realize that I need their ongoing support. Maybe I've given them the impression that I'm strong and can manage without help. Or maybe they don't know how to help. I guess it's time I have a heart-to-heart talk with the friends who mean the most to me. I'll tell them I recognize that our friendship is changing. I'll tell them what I'd like from them. With an open mind and heart, I'll ask what they would like from me to keep our friendship strong.

I treasure my friends
and I take steps to keep my friendships strong.

No Easy Answers

People don't understand. They say to do this or that, and it will all work out. Don't they see I've tried almost everything imaginable? There just isn't an easy answer.

I know they're trying to help. I feel their love and concern behind their comments. That's what I have to listen to beyond their words. Because I do need to know that other people are eager to support me. If I don't find their suggestions useful, I don't waste time disputing them. I simply say thanks. But I still have to listen for new ideas because maybe something someone says will make sense. Maybe it will give me a piece of the answer. Or maybe it will just reassure me that I've tried all the things there are to try. Even that would be a comfort and keep me from going over the edge.

Others can't give me the answers,
but they can remind me of what I already know.

The Power of Love

Love will carry me through, I know it will. I rely on love, because I couldn't do a lot of what I'm doing now for any other reason.

Remembering to tap into my loving heart helps me through the hardest days. When I feel worn out, resentful, or discouraged, I stop—if just for a moment—to reconnect with my feelings of love. I care so deeply for my loved one that I am willing to do what it takes to provide the kind of support that is needed. When love directs my actions, my tasks feel lighter. I connect better with my loved one and with other people. I feel right with the world.

*I am grateful that I have
the sustaining power of love within me.*

What's Changing?

Again and again, I'm taken aback when my loved one's condition goes through yet another change. I wish things would just settle down into a predictable rhythm.

But chances are, that will never happen. However, as I learn more about his condition and observe the changes in him over time, I may be able to see some patterns. When I note the first signs of a change, I can prepare myself and take steps to minimize their jarring effects on me. If I observe my thoughts closely, I might notice that I'm reluctant to prepare for difficult changes because I'm determined to maintain a positive outlook. I don't want to admit that something is about to go wrong. In the end, staying realistic and optimistic is a balancing act. Maybe even using those labels is artificial. I just want to stay attentive to what's happening and respond with care and competence.

I stay aware and flexible
to navigate this sea of change.

Wanting Tender Moments

I've heard about families having a reconciling experience in the midst of a family member's illness. People who have long been estranged suddenly make peace. I wish I could have a tender moment like that in my family.

But it may not be that way for me. My loved one may die without ever giving me what I want. And other members of my family may never be able to express their care in ways I would like. If a tender moment happens, it will most likely come from within my own heart. I will come to a point where I decide to love and accept my family as they are. I will see the basic goodness in them amidst all their disappointing behavior. If one of them responds with a touch or a smile or a kind word, that will be frosting.

I love my family members as they are.

When to Take Charge

I'd like to help my loved one, but I'm not sure what he wants. I wish he'd tell me what he needs, but he's not always able to do that.

When my loved one doesn't have the energy or know-how to figure out what he needs, or to ask for it, I take charge. I look around at what there is to do and do what seems sensible. Yet I want to respect his preferences at the same time. It's a delicate balance to maintain. If I'm sensitively tuned in to him and to what's going on around him, I'll notice whether laundry needs to be done, a water glass needs filling, clothes need changing. If he's up to responding, I check in with him about what he wants, but I don't insist he spend energy giving me detailed directions. Sometimes I have to do the thinking for him and even push for things I know he'd want if he weren't so sick. I can never be sure I'm right, but I do the best I can.

I stay alert, ask questions,
and take charge as each situation requires.

Honest Feelings

With all the drama that happens surrounding my loved one's condition, my feelings get very intense. The sadness, the shock, the resentment—they all mount up and just about knock me over. I don't always want others to know how I'm feeling, but I have a hard time holding it all in.

I'm glad I've got my journal. I can put on paper what I'm feeling in privacy. No one else needs to know. I can be totally honest. I don't have to hold back. If I'm angry about how much I've had to give up because of my caregiving responsibilities, I can say so without restraint. It won't hurt anyone and I'll feel a sense of relief writing down what's been eating at me. I'm not sure why, but once a feeling is down on paper, it becomes lighter and I can go on.

My journal gives me the freedom to be honest.

I'm Sure I'm Right

I get angry at my loved one. There are many things I wish he would do differently. I try to explain a better way and yet I can't seem to convince him. I get so frustrated.

Even though I would like my loved one to change, I can't make that happen. The only person I can change is myself. No matter how right I am, no matter how foolish someone else is behaving, I'm not the final authority on how anyone else thinks or acts. If I don't get agreement from my loved one, I only make myself miserable by dwelling on that fact. What will make me feel more peaceful and sane is, as the saying goes, to "let go and let God." I ask for help in releasing my desire to control other people, I change what I can on my end, and I entrust the outcome to my Spiritual Power.

I let go of my need to be right.

Heart Wisdom

Some of the things I have to do as a caregiver are things I detest. They're unpleasant, monotonous, hard work, and unrewarding. I tense up at the very thought of having to do them one more time.

The funny part is, the more I tense up, the more difficult a task becomes and the more miserable I become in mind and body. What if I try an experiment? When the thought of this activity comes to mind, what if I stop for a moment and act from my heart instead of from my tension-producing thoughts? What if I gently shift my attention to some enjoyable memory and let the pleasant feelings I remember from that experience come up in my heart? They might make me smile. From inside those pleasant feelings, I can ask for some heart wisdom to help me approach the task with greater peace of mind.

I ask my heart for help when I face a difficult task.

Intimacy

People ask how I can give so much time and energy to caring for my loved one. I give them reasons: My desire to be helpful. My sense of duty. Because I have no choice. But I wonder myself how I'm able to keep going.

Maybe it has something to do with the rewards I get for what I'm doing. I get some relief from my feelings of guilt. I have a sense of repaying what I've been given. I feel worthwhile. I feel noble. I feel less lonely. But none of these rewards is enough of a reason. What brings me the greatest satisfaction is when I experience intimacy with my loved one. I cherish the close and honest connection with her. With our frequent, close, and sometimes awkward interactions, we're forced to let our guard down. We get to see all the good, the bad, and the ugly in each other. Stripped of pretension, our souls touch and our hearts open to each other.

I stay open to intimacy.

Laughter

I can get mighty somber caring for someone who is suffering so much. With all the running around I have to do, the home chores, and other tasks my loved one needs help with, I get worn out and and sink into a sour frame of mind. A frown gets engraved on my face.

If I forget how to smile and laugh, that's dangerous. I know I can't survive for long without my sense of humor. When I get too somber, it's time to watch a funny movie or to start calling friends until I find someone who's heard a new joke. I could even laugh at my own foibles—or at my own seriousness. How about wearing a clown nose, an animal mask, fake tattoos? I could draw funny faces, read cartoons, play with a baby—anything to brighten my day and give the laugh muscles some exercise. It's worth a try.

I'll step on my laugh accelerator today.

Secrets

I wonder if my loved one could ever forgive me if she knew some of the things I've done. I've had some terrible thoughts about her, and I've done things that could have been disastrous for her. I feel ashamed.

I tend to want to keep these things a secret. But they eat at me. They steal my peace of mind. I worry that someone will find out. And even if no one does, I know the truth about myself. Carrying these secrets is a heavy burden. But I don't have to carry them alone. Sharing them with a trusted friend or a counselor can lighten the load. They are part of my humanness. A supportive listener can help me get perspective on them, experience acceptance and forgiveness, and decide if telling my loved one about them is a good idea. Once the secrets are out, they tend to diminish in my mind. My fears have made them larger than they are.

I find forgiveness and freedom by revealing painful secrets to someone I trust.

My Religious Community

I hesitate to go to a regular gathering for prayer or worship even though the music and messages soothe my soul. It's comforting to be there, but I can't stay. In this safe and tender place, tremendous sadness, too long restrained, breaks loose. I can't hold back the tears. I slip out to my car and can barely see through the wetness to get home. It may be hours before the crying stops.

It's too much for me to stay and try to explain to everyone how tired I am, how much it hurts, how out of control everything seems. But I know it's good for me to go there from time to time. Even when I can't stay, I am cradled for a while by the sacred sounds and sights and silences. I feel the understanding, the hope, the eternal caring. The tears find release there, and the grief pours out, as it must. I don't have to hold on so tightly anymore.

I draw comfort from my religious community.

New Activities to Enjoy

I miss some of the enjoyable activities I used to do all the time. Now I have to spend a lot of my time caring for my loved one. Even when I have some idle periods between tending to her needs, my favorite activities don't fit well in those situations.

It is true my old activities are on hold for now, but I wonder if I could find some new activities that easily fit into those idle times. Perhaps I could read, write letters or e-mail messages, do crossword puzzles, do handwork, draw, write prayers, play a solo game, study something of interest, dream and imagine, do exercises, listen to music or books on tape or inspirational messages. There are many options. I can choose one and get started. I might even ask a friend to join me.

*Today I'll make a list of new activities I might enjoy
and make plans to begin one of them.*

Music

My mind gets on a downhill track sometimes. I get discouraged and disgruntled with all the challenges of caregiving. When I feel myself slipping into this gloomy state, I need a jump-start to get out of it. Otherwise, it might be a long slide down into depression.

One thing that helps is making music. Singing regularly with another person or with a group is sure to lift my spirits. When I'm alone, I can sing along with my records or tapes or songs I hear on the radio. I can sing on my own, too, making up the words or humming if I forget the lyrics. Just making an effort to get a song started, even if it's a sad or sappy song, starts me breathing deeper and feeling some energy moving through me. If I get into full voice, my whole body feels the positive effects. A song with inspirational lyrics boosts my spirits.

Music creates a sunrise in my soul.

Preventing Burnout

I go and go and go, doing a million things for my loved one and trying to keep up with the other demands in my life. I go until I'm burned out and then I crash. It's a crazy cycle and it doesn't make sense to keep doing this to myself.

I don't burn out over one thing. A succession of tensions builds up until I can't push myself one more minute. When does this cycle start? Is it when I begin to skip meals? Is it when I am with certain people? Is it when I get a headache? The earlier I notice the presence of tension, the earlier I can detour myself from potential burnout. My tendency will be to think I'm too busy to stop and do anything about it. Or the tension will feel so familiar that it seems like no big deal. But if I take steps to relieve the tension when it first shows up, I will save myself tons of time later and eliminate the high price I pay for burnout.

I watch for signs of tension and tend to them
before they multiply.

Deterioration

It's frightening to see my loved one deteriorate. I want to see improvement, but instead I see a change for the worse. I feel so sad for her, and afraid for myself, too. It hits too close to home. I see things go wrong in my body and I know that, sooner or later, I face deterioration myself.

It's true, I don't like what I see and what it means for me ultimately. I want to turn away. It's enough to face the losses with my loved one, let alone foresee a decline for myself. It is humbling. Since there is nowhere to hide from this awareness, I allow myself to gently let it settle in. I sit in quiet contemplation, my soul naked with the intimate discovery of my mortality. I can't quite grasp it, I shy away, yet it is a moment of truth. Remembering the limitations of my body, I am reminded that there are higher things for me to seek.

I treasure my life,
and I respect the mysteries of change.

Family Issues

My loved one's condition tends to bring out the worst in certain family members. Old rivalries get re-ignited. People get adamant about their opinions. A few people end up doing most of the work. I wish we could have some peace in the family.

Perhaps we're all scared and we go to familiar ground for safety. Everyone needs reassurance and time to adjust. Whatever I can do to ease my own fears and help ease the fears of others will take the edge off the situation. Compassionate listening might be a good place to start. I begin by writing in my journal as a way to "listen" to my own anxieties. Then I try to tune in to the concerns of others in the family. I don't have to agree, just care. From a caring stance, I'm in a better position to keep a level head and take into account everyone's point of view. I'm able to remain more peaceful, and maybe that will catch on.

Where I desire peace, I bring peace.

Every Little Thing

I have a long list of things I want done differently. So many things get done poorly or not at all, both by my loved one and by others involved in his care. I try to get on top of all of them, but they just keep piling up.

If I tackle them all at once, I get overwhelmed. And I become a nag by insisting that things be done right. I get worn out. Pretty soon, no one is listening and I get even more frustrated. I've always heard it's smart to pick your battles. That probably fits in this situation. So I'd best focus on the things I most want done and let the little things go. They don't matter much anyway. I'll probably get better cooperation from others, too, when I'm not continually nagging them about every little thing.

I pick the most important changes I want to happen and focus on them.

Disturbing Reminders

Being with my loved one is stressful when she's receiving medical care. It triggers memories of similar situations that were agonizing for me. I'm torn because I want to support my loved one, but I dread being in these circumstances.

Great love is called for in these types of situations—great love for her and for myself. Only when I become immersed in sincere love can I embrace the tension I feel and still tend to both of our needs. My heart can express the deep care I feel for my loved one and be present with her when that is critical for her well-being. But it's also important that I respect my feelings and find ways to give myself relief from their intensity. I can check with my loved one and with the professionals to see whether my presence is essential. I can also write in my journal, talk with a good friend, or do a meditative exercise to help me come to terms with my discomfort.

I embrace both my willingness and unwillingness to be with my loved one.

Personal Body Care

What my loved one has to endure is not only difficult, it can be humiliating. So often he has no privacy, even for his most personal bodily functions. At times I'm sure it's hard for him to have me present.

Of course, there are awkward feelings on both sides—his and mine. Yet, I can minimize his discomfort from lack of privacy by treating him as respectfully as possible. I can let him know I realize this is difficult for him. Tenderness and humor can go a long way to ease the strain. It might help to check with him to see if he has any preferences about how or when I do certain things and then do my best to honor his requests. When he feels bad for me because I have to do unpleasant things for him, I can reassure him by saying, "No big deal. It's okay." Most important, I can remember to do my part out of love. That will make it easier for both of us.

I respect my loved one's body and treat tenderly the feelings that arise from his lack of privacy.

Good Sense

I know what my loved one asks of me isn't always reasonable. Sometimes she does it just to make me feel guilty. Which I do. I think: If I don't try hard enough to please her, then I'm not a good person.

But I'll never be good enough to suit her. In fact I think she wants me to fall short so she can feel superior—I guess. I can't really know her reasons, and they're not important anyway. What's important is whether or not I get taken in by her demands and slide into the hole of abiding guilt. The fact is, I'm not obliged to do everything she wants of me. That won't make me good enough. I'm already good and I am in charge of choosing what I will give. I can tell her, "These are unreasonable demands and I won't go along with them." Unless I take ownership of my choices and allow myself to be satisfied with each one I make, guilt will rip my soul apart.

I do what feels right to me and that's good enough.

Doing a Lot of Things Right

It's easy for me to find fault with how I'm caring for my loved one. I can quickly name a list of things I wish I were doing better. I get kind of discouraged by the many ways I come up short.

If someone asked me what I'm doing right, I'm not sure I'd have an immediate answer. But if I think about it for a minute, I've done a lot of good things as a caregiver. I've handled many difficult decisions. I've located and checked out resources. I've taken on learning a lot of new things. I've offered comfort and shown my love in many other ways. I've spent days, weeks, months of my time just being there. I forget to give myself credit for all I'm doing. Once a day, it would be good to reflect on what I've done well for that day and feel satisfied.

> *I feel peaceful about all the ways*
> *I've helped my loved one today.*

Growing Love

I am grateful that I can support my loved one. I know her pain and losses must be difficult to bear, and I wish I could do more to provide her relief. I'm glad I can at least be of some help and comfort during these challenging times.

While I am weighed down some days by the burden of caregiving, I am also blessed by this opportunity. It calls for a great deal of unselfish giving on my part—a level of love that I hardly knew I was capable of. What sweet irony that my loved one's health problems have allowed me to drink deeper of the well of love. My heart fills with a mixture of compassion and appreciation, sorrow and joy. It's good to know I have so much love inside of me.

I am thankful for my growing love.

Full Participation

People sometimes ignore my loved one. Just because he isn't as capable as other people, they tend to talk past him and talk with me instead. It's an insult to his dignity and it bothers me.

I include my loved one in every conversation and activity I can. It may take more effort, but my deep love for him prompts me to do it. Other people may need some nudging to include him. My example can be helpful. Once others see how easily I respect and draw upon his capabilities and stay engaged with him, they get the hang of it. Including him whenever possible is so satisfying for him—and for me. He has a great deal to contribute and he deserves to participate in life as fully as he can. I don't want him to miss out, and I don't want anyone else to miss out on what he has to offer.

I support and enjoy my loved one's participation in life.

Unconditional Love

I'm learning more about love than I could ever imagine. My loved one cannot do what she once could, so the giving between us is no longer mutual. I am daily being called on to give the kind of love that doesn't assume there will be love in return.

Admittedly, on some days, I don't feel much love. In fact, there are days when I feel like walking away. But on those days, I remind myself that love is not limited by how I feel. Love is an enduring commitment, a bond, and a choice to honor that bond regardless of circumstances. It is a gift that comes up from inside my soul—the ultimate expression of my fullness as a human being. It is my enduring link to my loved one and to all of creation. This pulsing energy called love is what keeps the world going, what keeps me going, and I am grateful for it.

Love lives in me, and I celebrate it today.

Surrender to a Spiritual Power

Some days it seems like everything I try to do goes wrong. I become an emotional wreck. I don't know where to turn. I feel like a failure.

On days like these, I know there is only one thing that brings me any real peace. When I've tried all the ways I know to turn things around without success, I finally turn to my Spiritual Power and surrender. I may have to ask for support from a friend or spiritual guide to help me do that, but when I finally let go of the struggle, a higher grace takes over my mind and emotions. On my better days, I remember to do that before I get desperate.

I let go of my limited and ineffective ways
and rely on my Spiritual Power to direct me.

Gnawing Problems

I sometimes get a problem in my mind that won't go away. I turn it over and over and see no way out. It keeps gnawing at me and I get more and more upset, but nothing changes. The problem remains.

However, when I get out my journal and start to write about my problem, I notice that I'm more likely to start moving toward a solution. Just the act of listing the issues gives me some clarity. Then I let my imagination loose and put down every helpful idea that comes to mind, no matter how far-fetched or unlikely. I start to see I have options. The logjam in my mind is freed up. Then I jot down the pros and cons of the various options, and before long, I'm moving from thinking about the problem to solving it.

On paper, my problems become more manageable.

Grateful for Growth

I don't know why I'm in this position of caregiver. I'm not prepared for it. I didn't ask for it. It has sidelined other things that are important to me and added hardship to my life. I'm tempted to feel sorry for myself.

Yet I know there is some reason for me to have this experience. There is something for me to learn. But even if I can't see beyond the struggle now, I trust that the good will show up over time. I know every experience in life offers a gift if I'm open to receiving it. Of course, I could also choose to make something positive come out of my circumstances. I have already learned a number of things, and I can look for opportunities to grow even more. It might help if I made a list of all the good things I've already gained as a caregiver and then choose one or two ways to build on them.

I'm grateful I'm growing.

Hurting Heart

Some days I care so much, my heart hurts. My loved one is in such misery. I would do anything to take the pain away but I can't. All I can do is to be there, show I care, and feel the ache inside my heart.

I've learned a lot about love during this time. My heart is pumping out a mixture of sweet joy, deep compassion, and wrenching sadness, all mixed together. At times I feel like these feelings will swallow me and I want to escape, but I can't run away from myself. These are my genuine feelings. They are part of me, they are the heart of me. They won't swallow me up, they'll just wash through me if I stay open to them. I'm willing to make room for more love in my life.

I let my feelings, big as they are, bless me
and teach me about love.

Asking Questions

I don't always understand what is going on with my loved one's tests and treatments. The various professionals all have their own lingo and although I try to understand, I can't keep everything straight. I feel frustrated and inept when I don't have adequate information to make decisions or help my loved one make them.

I may not understand everything, but I'm doing the best I can. I can always ask for further information or clarification. Even if I've been told once or twice before, it's okay to ask again. It's the professional's job to make sure I have the information I need. I won't let anyone talk down to me or leave me out of decisions that I should be a part of. I'm the expert on my loved one's personal needs and preferences. I exercise my love and authority to find out what I need to know and to have a say in matters that affect my loved one and me.

I ask questions until I know what I need to know.

Coming Apart

Sometimes I feel like I'm coming apart. Crises, changes, and decisions tug at me from every direction. I barely get one problem handled, when two more show up.

When I'm in that state, it's as if my energy is being scattered all about, moving away from me, pulling me with it every which way. If I closed my eyes and pictured that energy as several children tugging on me at once, I might imagine myself sitting down and gathering all those children close to me for a little chat, asking them to quiet down for a few minutes. I might sing a lullaby to get their attention. Then, in my mind, I reassure them that I intend to take care of each of them in turn. By quieting and reassuring all my different energy "children," I restore a sense of calm and order and direction. Then I can take care of each matter, one at a time.

When I feel pulled apart, I quiet myself
and gather in my energy.

Failures

I wish I could do more for my loved one. I've tried everything I know to give him the kind of help he needs. I've worn myself out running around making arrangements and getting things set up for him. I'm there with him as much as I can be. Yet I feel like I've failed him.

I don't know that I *could* do any more. Maybe I don't have to. How my loved one is doing is not totally in my hands. I can only do what I can do. I may not be getting all the results I want, but I have not failed. I have succeeded at giving all I could give and I'm glad I could give that much. Even if some things didn't work out, they were worth trying. I can be satisfied that I did what made sense to do. I don't want to second-guess decisions I've made. It will do no good. What is, is. I do not judge myself by outward successes or failures. I remember to appreciate myself for being willing to be there and to give what I can.

Each moment I give my loved one is a success.

Gratitude

On days when I can't find a positive thought to think, I need a way to lift myself up. When my thinking goes sour, I'm not much good for myself, let alone for my loved one. I need a day brightener.

When I'm in that state of mind, I try to think of something to be grateful for. That's almost guaranteed to get me started in an upward direction. I may have to look hard at first, starting with something very basic like, "I'm grateful I am able to move today," or "I'm grateful my eyes work or my hands work." It especially helps if I write down what I appreciate. Once I get a few items on my gratitude list, it's easy to come up with more. Pretty soon, the scales start to tip toward recognizing how much good is going on in my life and I get back in balance. There's more sweet than sour.

A gratitude list helps me remember
what is going well in my life.

Privilege

My loved one is very precious to me. I'm grateful to be able to be of help. As hard as it has been to watch her suffer, I am in awe of her resilient spirit and how she has come to terms with her condition.

Over and over she has had to face pain and setbacks and losses, and yet she finds a way to deal with them. I've seen her brave her fears time and time again. I've watched as she held tightly to many things she was deeply attached to and then reached a point where she could let them go. I've seen how she has fought with her experiences and then found meaning in them. I am learning from her. My problems seem small by comparison, and she gives me courage to handle them.

I am privileged to be a companion
on my loved one's journey.

Index

a

---

b

c

d

e

g

h

i

m

n

O

P

S

t

u

v

w